From Boy to Blue
Becoming One of America's Finest

Steve Warneke

Library of Congress Cataloging-in-Publication Data is available upon
request.

ISBN: 0-9986419-0-1
ISBN-13: 978-0-9986419-0-4

ACKNOWLEDGMENTS

Thanks to my family for their support. This would never have been possible had they not always believed in me. Thanks also to my dear friend Kelley Ann Arnold, whose long hours and assistance will never be forgotten. My respect and appreciation also extends to the unbelievably talented police officers across the country who sacrifice themselves every day. Lastly, I want to express my gratitude to the Denver Police Department. Thank you for the opportunity to realize my dream of becoming a cop. Your entrusting me with such an amazing responsibility to serve and protect the great people of Denver was truly a privilege and an honor.

CONTENTS

PREFACE

Public perception of modern-day police officers is in a nosedive. After over fifteen years of service as a Denver Police officer, it's my opinion that most of the cause of this isn't because cops are corrupt. In fact, police officers are more patient, more understanding, more gentle, and better equipped to end things non-violently than ever before. The reason for the decline in perception I believe has several facets.

Firstly, there is a lack of public understanding about a police officer's job and responsibilities. People need to understand what the officers face every day and comprehend the training and policies of modern-day police departments. While it's true that not all policies and rules are the same across the different law enforcement agencies, there are general trends that apply to a great many of today's departments.

Secondly, the media fuels much of the distrust of police departments today. The more controversy, the better their ratings. Also, the media and police departments report stories differently. By nature, the media will put most anyone on television to tell their account of what happened as soon as an incident occurs. Conversely, the police usually have very little to say upfront. The police department doesn't report most of the facts until after a thorough investigation. By that time, it's yesterday's news. Sometimes there's a follow-up blurb about a story, but it usually doesn't get the kind of attention it did the day it happened.

In response to the public's concerns, police departments have beefed up their efforts. There is more accountability and transparency in this industry than ever before. Where there isn't these things it is almost always because police departments are protecting the integrity of any potential criminal case.

I'm excited to share my experiences with you. I believe by becoming personally transparent and sharing what I've been through, it will benefit the relationship between officers and the public. It will begin to heal a relationship that desperately needs repair. The public-police relationship has a direct correlation with the safety of the public as well as the safety of police officers. As the trust and mutual respect improves, so does the welfare of everyone involved. This is the ultimate goal of my book.

So, let me tell you about me.

Being a police officer changes your life. It changed mine forever. When I was first on the job I told everyone I was a cop. When in social circles or meeting someone for the first time, I would think, *Please ask me what I do… Please ask me what I do… Please ask me what I do.* It wasn't that I was arrogant or cocky about it, I was just proud to say it. "Oh, me? I'm a police officer. Yeah, it's a pretty fun job. Oh sure it's dangerous, but I don't think about it much." Very modest, yup, that was me.

Later in my career, I thought, *Please don't ask me what I do… Please don't ask me what I do… Please don't ask me what I do.* If someone did ask, I'd say something like, "Oh, me? I work in the public sector, but enough about me, how about this John guy over here…a pilot, eh? What's that like?"

It's not that I'm ashamed—it's just that I've learned my lesson about telling people I'm a cop. You see, most people don't thank me for my service and admire my bravery. Most people launch into some unsolicited story about the last "asshole cop" they came across. They usually include some details that, if true, mean the police officer had superhuman powers and threw the person 100 feet with just their pinky or was secretly working for the mafia.

"And then, the cop came up to my car and pulled me out of my window by my eyelashes. That's right, then he beat me with his baton right there on the side of the road! Just when I thought it was over, he spit on me and said, 'That'll teach you to speed!' Can you believe he did that all because I was going two miles an hour over the speed limit?"

I got tired of everyone's account of what some cop did to them or "their friend." It was as if somehow I was responsible for it all.

In the beginning, I would defend the police or explain why cops acted the way they do (hint: it's all in their training). But it's hard to defend someone when you're only getting one side of the story—and, judging by the details, a very skewed version at that. In the end, people just wanted to tell their story.

"When can the cops go through my house or come in without a warrant?" Most people generally like to know about the rules of law that affect their lives. I don't cover all of them, but there's enough background on police procedures and our basic thought process to give most reasonable people an appreciation for our actions.

As you read, you will discover it is usually not a single, traumatic event that changes a man into an officer; rather, it's night after night of seeing the most unbelievable things. After all, there is no telling what any night has in store for us. We've seen a whole different side of the world.

I saw a guy shot right above the eye one night. He seemed fine—he was walking around and talking. He went to the hospital and they took an x-ray and decided to leave the bullet in his head. He went on with his life like nothing had happened.

I've seen other people shot in the low abdomen with a .22 caliber round that ended up dying in the ambulance on the way to the hospital.

I've seen what it looks like after several gang members in a car open fire on a family in their front lawn—and only one grazing wound to a man's calf. Amazing.

I've seen robberies, caught burglars, seen children killed by the very ones who are supposed to care for them.

I've seen children raped, even some by family members.

I've seen people beaten, kidnapped, stabbed, extorted, impersonated, burned…you name it and I've probably witnessed it.

I've also seen altruism on behalf of strangers, generosity, love, compassion, humor, and true heroism. Some of it involved the actions of other officers, and some of it was just a caring citizen.

You can't see this kind of thing day in and day out without it changing your life forever. Not every story in my career is unbelievably riveting or amazing, but the sum of these experiences begins to shed light on the reality of being a police officer.

By the end of this book, I hope you'll see that I'm not asking for zero accountability for the police force; instead, I'm asking for people to understand the complex nature of the job, the sheer number of things to consider on any call, the training we receive, and the number of different layers of oversight we already have.

Lastly, I wanted to share what I've been through. These stories make my jaw drop in amazement, make me angry, make me laugh out loud, and make me sob uncontrollably. I've felt many emotions as a police officer, and I want you to know about my life and my experiences. Maybe you'll come to understand the police better, or maybe you'll relate to some of these situations. My goal with this text is to change the way you think about the police and make your next encounter with them safer for everyone.

1
CHANGING OF THE MENTAL GUARDS

My mom once told me I couldn't spend my whole life driving around in fast cars, hanging out with my buddies, getting into fights, and listening to rock and roll. Boy, did I prove her wrong. Despite the fun times I had as a cop, this job elicited every emotion in me known to man. Someone once told me that being a cop is 98 percent boredom and 2 percent sheer terror. Police work is an unusual beast, and once it flows through your veins, I'm not sure if anything short of a transfusion of formaldehyde will stop it. I've met old, former, and retired cops and this mentality we all develop only seems to sharpen with time.

They call this job a ticket to the greatest show on earth, and the ticket is fastened to my chest every day. It's shiny and new. In the beginning of my career, it might have appeared I was a bit narcissistic because I was always looking at myself in the mirror. I wasn't so much admiring myself, but rather I was staring at my badge and neatly pressed uniform, relishing in what I had finally accomplished. It's that badge that will be the

VIP pass to many of the highest profile events occurring in any city.

The police department operations manual states the badge, gun and identification card is to be "on your person" at all times—which, when I was just starting my career, was no problem. A new cop never forgets any of these things. If I could have pinned my badge to my bare chest while I slept, I would have.

As I got a little older and more experienced, though, it just became a pain in the ass. State law and our operations manual grant us full police authority—twenty-four hours a day, seven days a week. Arrests can be made on or off-duty, and yes, even at the store when shopping for clothes. I didn't just *work* as a cop, I had *become* one.

Cops are told that our private lives must be "unsullied." In other words, I couldn't work at strip joints, own an establishment that needs a liquor license, my bills needed to be paid on time, and I needed to be free of liens and creditors. Approval must be granted for any work outside the department. It had to be approved by everyone from the sergeant to the chief of police. The administration wants to know what everyone is doing at all times and why.

Cops are required to always be "fit for duty." For example, cops are never supposed to be drunk. It's a ridiculous rule. How can you tell someone they *can't ever* get drunk? Under any circumstances, this job requires much more than the average position. It's a tremendous honor and yet an unparalleled responsibility.

I'm not going to lie—the power is luring for sure, but for me that was only part of it. Ever since I could remember, I wanted to be a cop. My parents thought this was a cute phase, and were sure it would pass. Eventually my father just started telling people I was going to be a doctor, hoping that the power of suggestion would pressure me into medical school. I let him run with that for a few years. When I got older, I finally told everyone I was still planning on becoming a police officer. My Aunt Fern would say, "What happened to the doctor thing, honey? You would be such a great doctor." Perhaps I would have, but I had already made up my mind.

Growing up, I watched all the cop shows, and was a cop for Halloween almost every year. The neighbors would say to each other, "Oh, look dear. It's Crockett from *Miami Vice*, and he's wearing the same white jacket and pants he did last year." The rest of the year, I was always being nosy in police situations. I would circle the block once if a cop had somebody pulled over just to see what was happening, and to make sure he was alright.

When a cop would go by me code 10 (that's the terminology for having your lights and siren activated) I could only slowly murmur a "Wooow." It was the same reaction that most people would have if they were to look at Earth from the space station. When cops had their cars in a 69 in a parking lot (parked front to rear so the two driver's side windows are together), I always wondered what they were doing or who they were talking about—and just so you know, it's not all top-secret stuff.

I spent years studying and preparing to enter the force. These years I spent testing and trying to get hired, praying, hoping, and crying at the frustration and the wait. It took me almost two years to get hired from the time I turned in my application until the time they called with the job offer. (That's not counting the years before my application that I stayed out of trouble and drove the speed limit so I didn't ruin my chances.)

My dream finally came to fruition. It was exciting and scary, but I knew I had to do it. Even years after being hired, I would occasionally catch my reflection as my police car passed by the windows of a business, and it still made me smile. I would always say, "I can't believe I'm the police."

The external changes were easy to see. Anyone can spot a cop from a mile away. The internal ones crept into my life slowly, like the way a puppy grows into a dog and you never notice it getting any bigger. Try to imagine yourself becoming more aware and more concerned about different things. You start to notice you're more alert of people, cars, or hazards. You start to see potential dangers, and you don't always think the best of people.

There are a lot of nuances cops are taught. These safety measures that cops acquire during their training and first few years on the job really start to annoy you in your free time. For example, *don't carry anything in your gun hand.* The academy drills this into every new recruit's head. Drinks, books, clipboards, phones, radios…nothing should be in that hand but air. The gun hand must be free at all times. It's a rarity to catch a cop holding his cup of coffee in his gun hand on or off duty. This is all well and good until I find myself trying to carry forty grocery bags into the house with just my left hand. I don't even realize I'm doing it until it occurs to me that my left fingers are about to snap off and my right hand is totally free.

Us cops don't like to sit with our backs to the door at a restaurant. "I'll take that table over there in the corner," I'll tell the hostess. Then I make sure to get the seat where my back is in the corner. Fine, right? Yes, until I'm on a date and I have to sit down last and end up with my back to the entrance. It causes a panic attack.

"Could we switch seats, honey?" I ask, nicely trying not to show my panic.

"Sure we can," says my date. I try not to imagine that they're thinking, *Great. I'm dating Jack Nicholson from* As Good As It Gets.

I hated having the dome light on in the police car after dark. That illuminated me and made a nice silhouette of my upper body and head, making me an easy target. Most cops rely on a flexible map light that hovers a couple inches away from the clipboard. After a while of this, the dome light made me nervous, even in my personal car off duty.

I pay more attention to my surroundings, even when I'm not at work. This is cool, until I'm walking the dogs and all I can think about is if somebody starts shooting at me, that tree over there will make for good cover…or, I wonder if anyone's on that roof? These things slowly permeate their way into everyday life.

In the academy, they teach everyone this saying: hands, weapons, footing, associates, cover, and escape routes. These are the things cops have to constantly be aware of. What does all that mean?

Hands: If anyone is going to hurt you, they have to do it in some way or another with their hands. A gun needs a hand to hold it and pull the trigger. (I suppose an exception to this could be if someone jumped through the air and wrapped their legs around your neck and choked you to death with their thighs like Jackie Chan, but I have to play the probabilities here.)

Weapons: Is there a gun or a knife? Is there any place on this person where a weapon could be hiding? Knives and guns are the obvious ones, but what about bats, crowbars, pens, razors, shanks, chemicals, needles, and so on?

Footing: Are you on ice, gravel, cement, dirt, or pavement? Is it smooth, rough, bumpy, slippery, or uphill? Will you have good traction when you run? Will the suspect have the same?

Associates: This is like an accomplice. Who is with the suspect? Could there be someone close by—a lookout perhaps? Maybe there's an idling getaway vehicle. Who else could be associated with this person?

Cover: Where can you go to take cover? What's close by? Will it stop a bullet? Trees, cars, and buildings probably will. Fences, doors, and interior walls probably will not.

Escape routes: If this situation gets too bad and you need to get out, is there a place to go? Can you get in the car and leave? Can you run away, and if so, where? How far do you have to run? Will you be exposed as you flee? If you escape, can the suspect escape the same way?

These are legitimate concerns for any officer. Not only that—they all have to be assessed instantly and simultaneously. Surprisingly, this behavior becomes fairly automatic…but it's exhausting. It's even more so when cops are doing this constantly on and off duty.

For cops who work at night, it's common practice to extinguish all lights, including the headlights, when getting close to a call. Even though it's a difficult task to hide a big white police car with lights on the top and reflective badges on it, we do the best we can with what we have. It actually works fairly well. You would be surprised at the number of people who fail to see us coming, simply by driving with our headlights off.

The problem came when I caught myself doing this in my regular car. Sometimes I extinguished my lights as I turned onto my street to go home. Unfortunately the location of the headlights in the police car happened to be the control for my windshield wipers in my personal car. I frequently had passengers inquire why, on a completely dry night, I activated the windshield wipers as we turned on my street to go home.

Along with extinguishing the headlights, cops try to always take off the seatbelt when getting close to the destination. There might be a need to have to get out of the car in a hurry. Maybe it's to chase someone, or maybe someone is charging toward the car. The bottom line is there wouldn't be a worse feeling than needing to jump out of the car in a hurry only to realize the seatbelt is still fastened. To this day, I still pop off my seatbelt about two blocks from the house. Try to imagine all this together. I'm driving along, pop my seatbelt off, turn the windshield wipers on, realize my mistake, and then turn the headlights off. Passengers think I'm nuts.

Another police practice is to never park in front of the house to which we are responding. The obvious reason is so someone inside wouldn't see me when I pulled up and start shooting from inside the house. Other reasons not to announce my arrival were to avoid scaring off any potential suspects, or letting the suspect get away by giving him or her a head start, and I certainly didn't want to create a hostage situation.

Sometimes, when parking far away and walking up on foot, it's easier to hear what's going on inside a house. These clues are important on any call. It could be something obvious like an argument or glass breaking, or it could be something more subtle but still important, like how many people are inside a residence.

And there's still more. Listen outside the door before knocking. Don't just walk up and bang on the door as if to say, "Trick or treat!" And another fun little habit all cops are taught: Don't stand in front of the door. It's just common sense. What if I knock and they shoot through the door? In my personal life, the problem then quickly arises that nobody I visit knows I'm there. They think it's a ding-dong ditch. I knock and my friend looks out the peephole, assumes kids are messing around, and returns to whatever he was doing. Thankfully, this usually doesn't continue for too long before he realizes it's his over-paranoid officer friend wanting to come play. My friends learned to expect this of me.

These are just a fraction of the things I did, no matter if I was at work responding to the call of a domestic, or going to pick up eggs at the local 7-11. You may not think all this is necessary, but that's because you imagine that it wouldn't be necessary when the police are dealing with *you*.

"I would never hurt a cop," you say to yourself as the police treat you like Lee Harvey Oswald. The problem is that the police officer you're dealing with doesn't know you. Wait until you hear about some of the people that cops have to deal with on a regular basis. Then, you tell me if you still believe all this isn't necessary.

As I explain some of my experiences, you might start to understand why it is we think this way. The paradox is that it's a good thing to understand, yet I wouldn't wish this constant state of doubting and paranoia, eternal questioning, and watching on anyone. The mindset of a police officer may be a curse, but it may save you from being a victim. It may be a godsend or it may be your worst nightmare.

However you regard the change, my hope is that you will reevaluate your thought process with regard to police officers and their work. By reading on with an open mind and not prejudging, you will be able to understand. This understanding will help heal the tattered relationship between citizens and their officers. You will be exposed to a world that you only hear about through the evening news. So take the plunge, but beware—you may not be the same afterward.

2
THE FITTING ROOM

There was significant sacrifice long before the hiring process began. Not hanging around drugs, never stealing or fighting were all part of the deal. I tried pot a few times, but stopped long before applying because I knew it had to be several years since one had done drugs in order to be hired. I walked a higher path—not a perfect one, but a higher one.

When the process began, I was ready for it. The application packet was extensive. It was thirty pages of desired information about me that not only did I not remember, but had a hard time finding out. Excuse me for not knowing who my neighbors were at every place I had lived over the last decade. The packet wanted to know anytime I was ever close to getting in trouble, the dates of any traffic tickets, any time a cop questioned me, and contact information of past employers and co-workers, friends, family, and relatives. It asked about landlords, lawsuits, and drug use, plus the dates, times, and places. I had to dig into my past to answer everything. This wasn't a task that could be done over a cappuccino at the local Starbucks.

The second phase of the process was the written test, which proved not to be too difficult. There was basic math, spelling, reading comprehension, and common sense questions. For me, it was an easy test.

The oral board followed the written exam. This was where I had to answer questions in front of a panel of people, some of whom were in uniform (talk about intimidating). It would be one thing to talk to normal, everyday people, but you throw a couple cops in the mix and I was just as scared as if I had been pulled over. One of the panel members would ask a question then start a stopwatch. Never mind any social graces like nodding along in agreement. They all simply stared in my direction. It was hard to tell if they were even breathing. There was a two- or three-minute time limit on each question and when I was finished, the only response would be from one of them who would ask, "Does that complete your answer?"

When I thought it was over, they were just getting warmed up. They had me talk to a psychiatrist and complete a written psychological test that asked, in about a hundred different ways, if I heard voices or thought I had been abducted by aliens. Those were the easy "No's" but then there were the questions like, "Do you talk to yourself?" I do, but I wasn't sure if that was okay. The psychiatrist interview was easy, although it was intimidating to be sitting in front of a doctor who was evaluating every answer to determine my sanity. He would ask a question then peer at me through the corners of his eyes as if he had flipped over the Tarot card that showed I was doomed.

There was the physiological testing like the drug screening and physical examination. "Turn your head and cough," said the woman doctor—which, by the way, that was the first and only time I had a woman doctor do that to me.

"It's pretty cold in here," I mumbled in between coughs.

When I went to the drug screening, they didn't just hand me a cup and tell me to pee in it. No, instead, someone had to come into the bathroom to make sure I actually peed and didn't whip out a cup of urine I had stashed in my pocket.

As if that weren't enough, they put me through a polygraph test. That was a horrific experience for me. I know this will sound strange, but there is nothing I hate more than having a blood pressure cuff on me. It's an idiosyncrasy of mine for sure, but the feeling of the inflated cuff around my arm makes me squirm like a fish out of water. Then when I start to feel my pulse from underneath the cuff, it's as if the blood is about to blow out of my arm at any moment. In a normal doctor's office, this discomfort only lasts for a few seconds. Try being strapped into a polygraph machine with that cuff on for what seems like an eternity.

Prior to hooking this contraption up, some guy asks a bunch of questions. Not just normal questions, but ones like, "Have you ever watched anyone else have sex?" I hadn't, but it sure sounded interesting. He also asked about gambling. How much money had I lost in a day? Had I ever taken out a loan to gamble? Then there were the drug use questions, which went on and on. Since I had tried pot, he wanted to know what dates I tried it, if I bought it, and how I obtained it.

After the whole interview, the examiner then hooked me up to the machine. He told me now he was going to have me lie on purpose. We went through some simple questions, and then he told me which question I was to lie about. After that was over, he said, "Okay, now I know what it looks like when you lie."

When the interview started, he asked, "Were you telling the truth in regard to all the questions I asked about sex?"

So on and so forth about each of the previously discussed topics. The whole thing seemed pretty hokey.

Looking back, I think it's more of a bluff. As the little needles go up and down, it is difficult not to watch them with the examiner wondering if everything is alright. My theory—now that I've been through this—is that they pick a couple of random areas (or the ones they think might not be true based on their own visual observations) and then say something like, "It doesn't appear as if you're being completely truthful in this area."

If people are lying, they assume the examiner knows. They figure they've been caught by "the machine." Figuring the jig is up, the testee then blurts out, "Oh, I forgot about the thousand dollars I stole from my former employer. I didn't know you wanted to know about that." Once caught lying, there is sufficient grounds to weed someone out of the process. Luckily for me, I was probably too honest, telling them every little obscure wrong I had ever perpetrated. The bottom line is I passed, and deservedly so.

The final phase was to assign a detective to snoop into my past. He talked to the references I provided, and then asked those references for other people who knew me. The second round of people was asked for a third, and so on. The goal was to find someone who didn't like me very much.

Anyone can get three people to say how great a person is. These are usually close friends and acquaintances. This background process takes quite a while, and during the whole thing, people I hadn't talked to in years called me to tell me some detective just came around asking questions about me, to which I would reply, "Really? That's interesting. So, ah, what did you tell them?"

Then one day I was driving home from work, and wasn't in a particularly good mood, when my cell phone rang. I didn't recognize the number, but answered it anyway in the snotty type of tone one would expect a telemarketer to be greeted with. The nasally woman on the other end of the phone said, "We're offering you a job at the police department if you still want it. So do you?" I was expected to give an answer immediately. So I told her, "Yes. Of course." The woman then gave me seven days to quit my job and report to my new one. Nice notice.

I arrived for the first day of the academy several hours early. I had prepared for multiple flat tires, traffic jams, being involved in an accident, going to the hospital, being treated and released and still being able to arrive on time. I paced around outside waiting for the doors to open, trying not to put a single wrinkle in my suit or spill one drop of coffee on me. I kept wondering when we would be issued our uniforms.

Jerry Seinfeld once talked about how much he hated clothes. Every morning, it's a task to have to pick out things that match, and make sure they're clean and ironed. Seinfeld said that as a society, we should pick out a uniform and vote on it so we don't have to dress ourselves everyday.

I agree. I would soon come to love wearing my uniform every day. I didn't buy clothes for years after the academy. On my days off, I wore sweats no matter if I was just laying around the house or if I was going out. It wasn't until I started dating again that I realized I would need to update my wardrobe.

In the academy we were required to wear the standard issue navy blue 1970s polyester pants and gun belt with all the bells and whistles (except we weren't given any bullets). The shirt, instead of the standard shirt worn by real cops, was a light blue short-sleeved shirt. The purpose of this was so we knew we hadn't made it yet. These shirts were smelly, old, and so thin from all the wear that strippers could have used them to show off some nipple. I wondered if Betsy Ross had been relegated to making them after completing the flag. I tried to wash my uniform, but even after five times, with enough detergent to make the shirt stand on its own, I was only able to mask the odor temporarily. We were not given a badge, but instead a patch was sewn on the left chest, identifying our status as a peon recruit.

The first week of the academy, the staff, in their torturous wisdom, gave us the real navy blue shirts we were going to get to wear after graduation. We were to take these shirts home, have them tailored, cleaned, and then put in the closet to gather dust. That was the catch—we were forbidden to wear them until graduation—*if* we graduated. So, of course I took them straight to the dry cleaners where I paid an extra $40 to have them completed in the next hour. I pretty much waited outside for them to be done, and when they were,

I took them straight home. I needed to put them on—to make sure they fit of course.

I waited until everyone in my house was gone before I started the unbelievably complicated dressing ritual that would soon become routine. I call it a ritual because it really is just that. There is so much shit to put on, and in pockets, that it's impossible to achieve perfection on the first few attempts. Not only that, but as I would come to find out, it takes a good year of rearranging everything to get it where you want it. I found equipment would dig into my hip, or some things were needed more often than others. You don't want the tools you use the most to be all the way around, in the small of your back.

Equipment placement is an exact science. For the first month I was on the streets, my backup gun lined up perfectly with the tiny panic button on the top of the police radio. As the button was depressed, this would cause a city-wide simulcast saying that I was in trouble when I wasn't.

I found a different spot for my radio.

Trying all this stuff on the first time was difficult. I finally finished four hours later, after dressing and undressing several times. The uniform was now complete, all except the badge. I went upstairs to my father's full-length mirror in the bathroom and stood there in silence for what must have been the better part of the day. Part of me thought, *What the hell did I get myself into?* The other part of me just kept repeating, *Oh my God, I'm the police.*

The nervousness I felt stuck with me for the rest of the afternoon. This feeling only intensified over the evening. With every recollection of myself in the mirror came another wave of nausea. I was sitting at the dinner table that night unable to eat anything, when I felt it coming. I beelined it for the bathroom and threw up what little food I had force fed myself at dinner, looked up into the bathroom mirror with my watering eyes, and said out loud, "I'm the police."

I took a couple deep breaths and thought the first thing I have to learn is how to remain calm.

3
RED MAN

The academy was twenty-one weeks of torture.

None of us wanted to be in classrooms; we wanted to be out on the street. We didn't want to learn verbal judo; we wanted to be chasing down bad guys. Looking back now, sometimes I wish I could go through it again so I could work Monday through Friday 7:00 AM to 3:00 PM with weekends off. I could use the break now. Sure, we had our driving days, shooting days, and days on the mat learning to fight, but they didn't seem to come often enough.

The academy staff tried to weed people out by telling us we were quitters and to go back to our other jobs before we got hurt or killed. At the time, I was wondering why they weren't trying to motivate us more. Why were they so negative? Shouldn't they be telling us to give it the old college try?

After I had completed the academy and had been a police officer a while, I understand that the people who don't really want this, or who are scared to do this job, are more likely to quit under those circumstances. This is exactly what is desired because if I were in a fight for my life out on the street, I wouldn't want my partner to decide that this wasn't for him and go lock himself in the car. I want to know that the person next to me persevered through what I did, and proved they have what it takes to be next to me.

I grew up in the suburbs. I had been in two fights in my entire life, and they were hardly knock-down-drag-out brawls. The first of them I won after slamming some kid's head into a brick wall. He had thrown sand in my face for no reason. I had never even met him. He wasn't hurt, didn't bleed, didn't even fall over. In fact, he chased me and I ran and hid in the boy's bathroom standing on top of a toilet until the teacher found me and brought us both to the principal's office.

The other fight was with a roommate at college while we were both drunk. Neither one of us can even remember what the argument was over. We wrestled around and put a quarter-size dent in the cheap bedroom door.

Growing up, I was hardly regarded as a pugilist. The only other experience I had with fighting was a brief stint in which I took karate. I was only a kid, and I dropped out after just a couple months. They taught me if someone punches with their right arm, you block it and then kick them here and punch them there. But after seeing a few fights with my own eyes, I determined that people don't fight with one left hook and then wait for the retaliation. The people I've seen in street fights like to brawl in what I call "monkey mode"—when a person just goes berserk, throwing punches with both hands while managing to kick with both legs in between the punches. Anything goes. Karate didn't seem to me to teach how to defend against that.

There was an initiation of sorts in the academy. It was called Red Man. At first, it seemed like nothing but an excuse for cops to beat up the new hires in some sort of sick, twisted hazing ritual. After it was over—and now that I reflect back on it—Red Man was a day that changed my life forever.

Not long after the academy began, gossip about Red Man surfaced. The rumors were that people were hospitalized and came out of the thing with various broken bones. I was terrified, and I'm sure everyone else was too. Some tried to hide their fear and act tough, but not me. I looked as nervous as I was. As people came back from their turn, I would interview them at length to see how bad it was while I physically examined them for injuries.

Red Man was set up as a three-minute scenario. It was one new recruit versus five or six academy staff members. We were retrieved from a classroom one by one and taken with an instructor into the gym. One purpose of this was to demonstrate just how long three minutes is when you are in a fight. As I would soon learn, it is an eternity.

"You are responding to a bar fight" is what the administrator told us as we entered, one by one. I then noticed several people wearing pads—full body suits of red padding, hence the name Red Man. Pads over the chest—like an umpire would wear in baseball—shin guards, arm guards, big mitts over the hands, and each person was wearing a helmet with a facemask. It was at this point I wondered why I had no padding.

As soon as my partner and I walked in, they were yelling at us, "Oh look. It's the cops. What are they going to do? Why don't you get the fuck out of here, you little pussy cop?" It sounded like a good idea to me, but there was no turning back.

As we entered the gym, one of them attacked the instructor posing as my partner, and tried to take his gun.

"He's got my gun! He's got my gun!" he yelled.

Charging at any red in sight, I tried to save my partner and stay on my feet as long as possible. I attempted to punch and hit them in the pads, but they would blindside me from behind, knocking me down.

"Get up, you little pussy!" one guy taunted.

They waited until I was dog tired. My punches at them became equivalent to being hit with a feather. Just when I was all out of gas, they knocked me over and then piled on top of me. One person was on each leg, another on my lower back, one was pulling my arm out from underneath me every time I tried to use it to get up. Someone else would slap me in the face or hit me in the ribs periodically, but all of them were talking shit.

"Why don't you go back to your little radio gig? You can't handle this. Why don't you give up?" They all tried to offer me a chance to give up, but I didn't.

Lesson two: Don't give up, ever. When fighting for your life, never quit. Do something, anything, find some way to keep fighting. Don't just lie there and succumb to death.

Just when I thought it couldn't get any worse, one of them started to cover my mouth and nose with their hand so I couldn't breathe. Black closed in all around me, and just as my vision narrowed to one pinhole, the hand would come off and I would gasp for breath. As soon as I could see, the hand would go back on again.

At one point, I began to wonder if they were really going to kill me and then play it off as an accident.

Everything—the covering of the mouth, the slapping and hitting, the shit talking, and the arm being pulled out from underneath me—continued until the whistle blew.

It took me several days to recover from this. I had a strange cough and other problems like headaches and mental cloudiness for a while after Red Man. (Not to mention that I wanted to find the guy who covered my mouth and slit his throat. I asked him a few days later how he knew when to take his hand off my mouth, and he told me that when my eyes started to flutter and roll back in my head, he would let go.)

After everyone had gone through Red Man, the staff picked out three people who put up the biggest fight—I was one of them. That's no small accomplishment for a scrawny suburban kid who had never really been in a fight. After all, there were thirty-two people in my class. When it was over, I still didn't understand why this was necessary. I wondered if the following week I would be forced to eat raw jalapenos and wash it down using a beer bong. The staff said the main reason for Red Man was to show what it felt like to lose a fight. That was the goal—we were to lose, and we all did.

"Remember what that feels like," one staff member told me, "because you never want to be in that position again." He also told me to "always remember just how fast things can go to shit." Nothing could have been truer. Come hell or high water, that was never going to happen to me again.

We also learned once criminals smell fear, they know they have won. Soon after the Red Man exercise, the staff showed us a video of a Georgia officer who was killed in a gunfight. To this day, that remains the most horrific clip of video in existence, especially since the officer had a chance to win the fight.

The man he had stopped for traffic got out of his car and was running around screaming. This guy was truly a nut-job. He went back to the car, got out a rifle, and began loading it. The cop only yelled orders at him. It was obvious in his voice he didn't know what to do and was utterly terrified. The officer tried to approach him then retreated. The man went on screaming and loading his rifle until he actually started shooting at the officer.

The cop was killed and if that weren't bad enough, I had to sit through the extended version of this video. The dash cam video kept recording after the shooting, when although all that could be seen was the hood of the patrol car, the officer's last gurgling breaths as his lungs filled with blood were caught on tape.

After the trial, to which the guy was found guilty and sentenced to prison, federal investigators asked the man why he killed the officer. He told them the trooper didn't have control over the situation. He could tell the cop wasn't sure what to do, and was scared. He said that if the officer had been more forceful, this probably wouldn't have escalated.

Even though the Georgia officer wasn't ambushed by several people in red pads, the lessons are the same: Things can go badly very quickly. Losing control is not only terrifying; it can prove to be fatal. An officer must be confident and willing to act using training and tactics.

Believe it or not, Red Man also built confidence. At the end of the academy, after all the training, Red Man was revisited. This time, we were equipped with all of our gear, all of our training, and armed with the fact that we didn't want to lose again. The second go-around is set up so that we win, and we all did. (Talk about a confidence builder.) The first Red Man still haunted me, though. With one hand over my mouth, all the invincibility that accompanied childhood disappeared. It was a valuable lesson, and one I'm convinced nobody should leave a police academy without.

I went back to the academy years later to assist the staff with the Red Man training of a new recruit class. Covering people's mouths or being too rough on them was no longer allowed. This coincides with the general trend in law enforcement of a kinder, gentler police force. That wouldn't be so bad...except on the street, criminals unfortunately aren't following that same trend.

4
MY FIRST CALL

I had just graduated the academy and been given my first assignment in the "Hollywood Division," a district known for its rich and affluent people. Everyone said that I would fit in well, since I was a pretty boy who looked more like I should be playing a cop on television than being a real one.

I was assigned my first field training officer (FTO). She had been an officer for nine years already. This fourteen-week field training program would prove to be the most demanding and stressful period of my life. It made the academy look like a vacation. Imagine your workday, but then add someone sitting right next to you watching and listening to your every movement and then grading it.

On a few occasions I would be driving to a call and going in the wrong direction, but not know it. My trainer just sat there in complete silence as if I were doing just fine, but soon I would start to suspect something was wrong.

"I'm not going the right way, am I?" I would ask, afraid of the answer.

"I don't know. Are you?" would be her calm response as she pulled out her pen to make note of my error. I would come to dread the sound of Velcro—that's the sound the shirt pocket made as it was pulled open, revealing the dreaded red spiral notebook.

Every day, there are many tasks to be done simultaneously: listening to the police radio, navigation, the actual driving, the approach, where to park, and what needs to be done on scene. Once I arrived, I would feel the cold stare of my training officer over my shoulder as I filled out each box on the report. I would try to distinguish each grunt as approving or disapproving. Was that grunt a *you just screwed up the whole thing* grunt? Or did it mean *good, but hurry up already. I'm hungry*? Speed in report writing comes with time, but as I would later come to find out as a trainer myself, it's frustrating to sit there and watch someone do something at one-eighth the speed any veteran can do it.

But report writing is only a small feat to accomplish. When cops are new, it's challenging to tell people to sit down or to stand in a certain spot when dealing with them, especially if you're used to customer service where the customer is always right.

Can you imagine selling someone a car, walking into the showroom and saying, "Put your hands on the car," then patting them all over including the groin only to finish by ordering, "Go sit over there on the couch and put your hands in your lap"?

My first day started off fine. I got the "here's what I expect of you" speech. When the little talk was over, we went outside to the car and my training officer told me to load my gear into the police car. When new recruits start this job, they have bags and bags of equipment. There are reports, and then a tote with extra reports in case the first ones run out. A good recruit also needs law books, procedure books, a whistle, scrap paper, chargers, jackets, long-johns, riot gear, traffic vests, hats, and a variety of other things only used once in a blue moon. After a few years, a veteran's duty equipment consists of a magazine, a book, maybe an iPad, and one clipboard with paperwork in it.

We conducted the vehicle inspection in the parking lot to make sure there was no new damage on the police unit before I began to load up all my things. I hadn't got the first bag out of my personal car when over the radio came the call of a burglary in progress. There was allegedly a group of Hispanic males kicking in the back door of a house.

"Quick! Leave your stuff. Let's go!" shouted my FTO. We jumped in the car—she was driving, thank God, because with all the adrenaline I couldn't have found the place with a GPS system. She pulled out of the station, turned on the lights and siren, and sped down the middle of the road over a painted median, dodging in and out of traffic, running red traffic lights and stop signs.

It's one thing to drive crazily when you're behind the wheel, yet it's another to have a complete stranger weaving in and out of traffic with your life in their hands. For some reason, they're never doing it as well as you would if you were the driver. I remember thinking that we weren't even going to make it there. Part of me wished we would crash on the way, so I wouldn't have to confront a gang of armed burglars. The other part of me wondered why is it we were driving *to* a gang of burglars when we should be driving *away* from them to a safe place where we could call the police. (This would be a question I would come to ask many times in the beginning of my career.) It is strange to think about, but if anyone told you of something horrific happening, where it was possible you could get hurt or killed, running *toward* the chaos would most likely be at the bottom of the list of your desired things to do.

When we arrived, I saw a group of Hispanic males in the backyard of a house. My field training officer, this woman I had been assigned to, was the one who was going to save me if I got in a fight for my life, and I would have the same responsibility if she were to get into trouble. I felt a connection with this woman like I hadn't felt with anyone else. She was my lifeline, and I was hers.

I once went bungee jumping, which was probably the stupidest thing I have ever done. It wasn't fun and I would never do it again. When I jumped off the tower I held the pad attached to the harness around me so tightly that if it had been a person I would have crushed them to death. That's what I felt like doing to my training officer when we got out of the car.

This would accomplish two things. First, it would make me feel safe, but second, it would provide me with a shield. Since this wasn't a possibility, I just kept going. My trainer approached the gang without fear, but with caution.

As it turned out, the "gang of burglars" was only a group of construction workers who were hired to remodel the house and were having a little fun in the demolition phase before the construction started.

I breathed a sigh of relief. I was ready to retire. I had done it, I had made the world safe. I could go on with my life knowing that I was the brave one who had risked my life for complete strangers who weren't even home when their back door was kicked in. But instead of being honored with a parade and a key to the city, we went back to the station, loaded up my things, and went to work. The only thing I had gained from my first call was a new family member: my trainer.

As time went on, I developed this same connection with many of my co-workers. Some of us went through something together, and with others, we just knew we wore the same color. My family began to grow, and just like a real family, I had some who I liked, some I didn't, but they were all kin.

I once participated in a trust-fall at one of my other ridiculous jobs growing up. The basic theory is that your co-workers stand behind you while you turn your back to them and fall backward, relying on them to catch you. As a cop, every call is a trust-fall, but the end result if it goes badly isn't a bruised tailbone, it's a wood coffin. It's this trust that quickly makes a cop's co-workers his whole world.

I hadn't exactly remained calm on my first call, but I would soon learn how to do this. It's easy to panic in stressful situations. People who are normally very bright seem to get tunnel vision and can't act or move when there's an emergency. I've become quite good at remaining calm in emergencies. It's difficult to explain, but when I feel the panic set in, I just take a deep breath and tell myself to slow down and think. After I do that, I'm calm, cool, and collected. This technique works well for me, but of course I get more emergencies to practice than the average person. Most people almost never get many life and death situations in which to try to remain calm.

After a few years on the job, a frantic woman called 9-1-1 and said the accelerator on her car was stuck and she couldn't stop. She was barreling down the highway and having to dodge traffic, even using the shoulders of the freeway to pass cars in an effort to avoid a collision. Apparently, the operator was trying to get the woman to put the car in neutral, or turn the car off, but she just couldn't. To stop her, two cops maneuvered a police car in front of her and slowed until she hit the back of their police car. The cops then used their brakes to slow both vehicles until they safely stopped on the highway. The story made national news.

I'm sure it must have been terrifying to be in a car that wouldn't stop. I know for a few seconds I would have panicked as well. The difference would be that after the initial panic, most cops would have been able to calm down and find a way to stop the car. It demonstrates—albeit to an extreme—how inexperienced the average person can be at handling life and death situations.

People in my life come to me on a personal level when there's chaos in their lives. They know they can count on me to be cool and level-headed. They know I will be able to give good advice and think clearly even if the circumstances warrant panic. It's a skill I'm glad I have developed. It may just save my life someday—and maybe it already has. Frankly, there isn't any other way of getting good at controlling adrenaline besides being faced with situations on a daily basis that make the butt pucker.

It may be just this reason that cops are so close. We all have been through many hair-raising events together. We know we need each other in order to survive, and we count on one another to exhibit this cool-headedness in emergencies.

The same can be found in people who aren't cops if they have survived a traumatic event together. Think about the survivors of any plane crash, hostage situation, or other major event. Those people form and maintain life-long relationships after making it through something together. Cops go through these kinds of events together all the time.

The department received a call of an intruder in the nicer area of town. It was a high rise apartment building that resembled more of a stuffy inner-city hotel. The doors were crowded together and the hallways were yellow with the tint of cigarette smoke. The smell of everyone's dirty laundry permeated the building. The sounds of classic television reruns like *I Love Lucy* and *Barney Miller* rose and fell through the halls as we passed the doors.

As we methodically made our way through the halls looking for the intruder, we got to the apartment and listened outside for a moment and didn't hear anything.

Elderly people have an uncanny knack of sensing when someone is at their door. Before we could knock and announce ourselves as police, the door opened a crack and an older white man peered through the slit, his gray, wiry hair looking as if he had just awakened from a month-long hibernation. His eyes were magnified from his glasses. His clothing was conservative, but soiled and disheveled.

"I want them Indians out of here. I told them to leave but they won't," he whispered to us. We entered the apartment fully expecting to find several Native Americans making smoke signals inside, but the place was empty. I asked where they were, thinking they may have retired for an afternoon snap (police terminology for a short nap).

"What's wrong with you? They're right there!" the old man barked. He then turned and pointed at an empty couch.

"How many of them are there?" I asked, a bit confused.

"Are you fucking blind? There's three of them!" he snarled. After a "Well, okay," the other officers and I searched the apartment, not necessarily looking for Indians, but looking for anyone else, dead or alive. This is done on most routine calls to determine if anyone else is in the house. It's never a good thing to have someone back in a bedroom doing God knows what while cops are out in the living room trying to deal with a problem.

This is called a protective sweep—and no, those of you who always tell tales of your credentials of being a law student, there is no need for a warrant, and here's why: When the police are lawfully on the premises, we conduct this "protective sweep" to ensure nobody comes charging out of the back room with a knife, or to make sure nobody is lying in a back room bleeding, clinging to life. Thankfully, nobody else was in the apartment, not even Indians.

We attempted to talk to the man who I learned had been retired from my police department for fifteen years, and there on his coffee table amid the dirty glasses, papers, ashtrays, and the remains of TV dinners was the man's badge. I spoke calmly, trying to comfort and convince him that he needed to go talk to somebody without saying the word "psychiatrist." I knew he was going to have to go with us one way or the other, but it's always nicer to make someone think the idea was theirs.

I'm so naïve! Here stands a twenty-five-year veteran of a big city department who has seen more than I had in my short stint on the job, and at the mere mention of going to talk to somebody, he saw right through my shallow attempt at telling him he was nuts.

"What, do you think I'm crazy, rookie? Fuck you," he said. Luckily for me, a sergeant was on scene, one with a lot more experience than me, and he was able to have a cop-to-cop talk with him and persuade him to go the hospital voluntarily, but not before the man jolted around and pointed at the small cement balcony and screamed, "There they go! Them crazy sons-a-bitches just jumped off the balcony and you're letting them get away!" (I felt the need to point out the apartment was fifteen stories in the air, but I refrained from sharing my little observation.)

To this day I don't know what the sergeant said to him. I know two things, though: I couldn't have listened in on the talk because my mere presence would have insulted the man and caused the sergeant's purpose to fail. Secondly, by the time the sergeant left with this guy, arms around each others' shoulders, this man truly believed in what the sergeant had said and went to the emergency room psych-ward just like he was asked. That's when I thought to myself, *Man, I've got to learn how to do that.*

Thus, my goal on every call became to take something from the experience. I took several things from this one. It was amazing to me that fifteen years after retiring, this man still kept his badge in plain view on the coffee table. I'm sure he had a place for it while he slept too. It occurred to me that for the most part, police officers are proud of who they are and what they've done. This isn't just a job, it's our identity. Everyone in society identifies with their job to a great extent, but this job seems to run much deeper.

I also began to wonder if the stress from this job would have me attempting to shoo away imaginary Indians from my living room in thirty years. I resolved then and there not to take my work home with me and to seek counseling at least a few months out of each year.

5
CRUEL AND UNUSUAL PUNISHMENT

For my first real burglary call, I had visions of screeching up in my patrol car with the lights flashing and siren wailing. As I'm jumping out of the car, pumping the action on the shotgun, the burglar comes running out the front door with a black face mask and a bag of jewelry, only for me to have him surrender and perhaps swear off crime forever because the mere intimidating presence of the police showed him the light. "Just doing my job," I humbly tell the thousands of people gathered at the ceremony to award my medals. Naturally, the president presides over the affair.

But as it turns out, it was a false alarm. In reality, ninety-nine percent of the alarm calls are unwarranted. In fact, it becomes so routine that commonly single-manned cars will "advise on cover." In other words, they go alone and promise to check back once they get there to say if they need a cover car, essentially handling the call by themselves. Sure, occasionally a business or a residence will have an open door. This will require at least two people to check the inside. Since most of the cars in my city are only staffed by one cop, a second car needs to respond.

Unfortunately, police work is reactive in nature. My action is determined by waiting to see what the opposition is going to do, and that puts us good guys at a disadvantage from the beginning. The bad guy knows if he's about to run. He has time to think about where to land a sucker punch. Criminals already have a gun ready as the cop walks up. But most calls don't involve this kind of high drama.

Complacency is dangerous, and we strive to fight it off, but to some degree it is inevitable. The longer a cop is on the job, the more difficult it becomes to keep at the full-ready. And since not every call ends up being dangerous, cops use any instance to keep ourselves prepared. That usually comes in the form of being hard on each other.

Cops can be a cruel bunch in-house, but we are family. What siblings don't give each other a hard time? Plus, we need to be resistant to words. The old *sticks and stones* adage applies here. People on the streets make fun of us, call us names, and say other things to get our goat. It's difficult to be taunted and teased by the people we protect. It's easy to get angry and frustrated in these situations. A cop must be resistant to this, however. We can't let anger blur our judgment or get the better of us. If it does, even once, it might mean the end of a career, and cops aren't meant to do anything else. Imagine how long I would last at the local grocery store handcuffing people for sampling grapes. Even being hard on each other serves a purpose by developing thick skin.

A couple years into my career at about three in the morning, a bunch of us were just getting ready to go meet at the Village Inn for our nightly meal. We were all hungry and tired when one of the guys I work with got an alarm call. It was one of the last calls one would want in that situation because it was an alarm at a huge office building across town. He knew that inevitably he was going to drive all the way out there just to end up walking around the entire base of this building, through bushes, pulling on doors to make sure they were secure. He'd also be checking for broken glass or anything else that seemed out of the ordinary. But chances were even if it was a real burglary, most likely it would be long over by the time he got there.

No matter what, even when everything appears undisturbed, there is always that little voice in the back of an officer's head whispering, "This might be the big one. This may be the time a burglar really is inside, or the bandit is waiting behind the next corner with a gun and a clean shot to my head." In the police force, every day has the possibility of being the day you have to fight to survive.

Just as it was scripted, it happened. He walked around yanking on locked doors in the dark of night. Just as the officer got to the last door, as the thought of hot pancakes and eggs surely came to his mind, he pulled the door and it opened. The office building was so large it would take Superman, with his X-ray vision, the better part of an hour to search. On every floor there were cubicles, and there was story after story of the same. There were desks, closets, bathrooms, stairwells, and other nooks and crannies all over the place.

After what I'm sure was a small temper tantrum after finding the open door, he called for a cover car. Now the other cops were even more irritated because one or more of us had to leave our freshly delivered hot meal to go help search this place, which, again I will remind you, is across town.

Imagine if you were his cover car. As you tiptoe through the building with your gun forging the way, you get about halfway through the building when out of nowhere you begin to hear rustling nearby. Is this the big one?

With the tension building just like a scene out of a low-grade horror movie, it happens. No, you don't throw your gun at an assailant and run out of the building screaming, which might be the layperson's reaction. You hear a loud noise as if something got knocked over. It's just like in *Die Hard,* but with a twist. Just as in the movie, the German antagonist leader has given the cue for the muscular seven-foot martial arts expert to kill you.

But this isn't the movies. You aren't Bruce Willis and you aren't waiting for this with the attitude of "Yippie-ki-yay motherfucker!" Instead, despite your best efforts, the only cowboy attitude you can muster is a small amount of pee slipping out.

As all of this is happening, from out of the corner of your eye, you see something moving right at you. Who is this? Why would they attack you? You're convinced they're trying to hurt you. You point your gun and shoot. *BANG!* The flash from the muzzle illuminates the room for a brief moment. After that fiery flash from the muzzle vanishes, you are temporarily blinded until your pupils can readjust.

Finally, as the room slowly comes back into focus, you assess your health wondering if you are still breathing. Have you been shot or stabbed? Did you win? Where is the guy who was wearing the hockey mask and the knife that you just shot? You didn't see him but you know he's got to be here somewhere.

You feel your heart beat in your throat and you know that's a good sign. That's when you look where the dead body should be, when what do you see but a small, cute putty-cat. She's proud and playful, and acts as if nothing has happened. She lifts her paw, licks it, and then uses it to clean her brow. Then it hits you: You just shot at a cat.

The cat isn't dead, so thoughts of PETA protesting outside your house late at night subside. Luckily for you, you weren't quite the sharpshooter your daydreams had made you out to be. Unluckily for you, you have just discharged your weapon on duty. The detectives will have to be called at home and woken up. After any discharge of a firearm while on duty, the homicide unit has to come out and investigate. The thought of salty, angry, old-time detectives being woken up in the middle of the night to come clean up your mess is worse than having to leave your hot meal behind.

It wasn't always like this. If this would have happened years prior, as long as nobody was hurt, a much simpler protocol was enough. It's seems like overkill, but unfortunately nowadays the department has to account for every round and what it hit.

Once detectives get there, those little yellow tents with numbers on them are set up, each one reminding you of how many stupid things you've done. Then photographs are taken, everything is collected, statements are written, and on and on goes the red tape for hours. You will be allowed to return to the station exhausted, hungry, and embarrassed only to find your comrades, your co-workers, your confidants are there to support you. They have managed to find, in the middle of the night, little toy stuffed kittens which have now been defaced with holes cut in them and X's over the eyes. Stuffed cats find their way into your mailbox, locker, and even your personal car. Catnip, balls of yarn, and other cat paraphernalia will be gifted to you for months and months to come. And yes, this happened exactly as I described to one of my coworkers. Cops can really be a cruel bunch.

If you talk to cops, they'll admit they can be hard on each other. Ask an old timer the logic behind this and they will say, "If you can't take it in the station, how are you going to take it on the street?" That logic seems second grade, but I must admit, it's true. Because of this, I don't get as angry about being teased or taunted. I can take a joke no matter the subject, and I can even make fun of myself. In fact, I've found the way to keep the ribbing to a minimum: Make the worst jokes about yourself, and there's nothing left for anyone else.

You'll begin to notice I refer to my unimpressive stature quite a bit. That's because I make no bones about it. I am not in the business of convincing everyone that even though I am 5'8" and 150 pounds, I am some ninth-degree black belt who is registered as a lethal weapon. The smartest thing anyone can realize about themselves is that no matter how big of a badass you actually are, there is always someone bigger and stronger.

Impressive or not, everyone has to take a ribbing for something. I once rode with a guy who was even smaller than me. He was probably 5'6" and 130 pounds. At roll call one day someone made a comment about the two of us together probably only weighing 150 pounds, which was greeted with a roar of laughter from everyone in the room. Instead of getting angry and telling everyone to shut up, which would have only prompted more heckling from the peanut gallery, I quickly added, "Yeah, I have to steer while he works the pedals." This was undoubtedly funnier than what had already been said, and was met with the corresponding increased laughter. I wasn't done yet, though. "Can someone lend us a couple of child seats so we can hit the street? Maybe if I stand on his shoulders, people will take us seriously!" Each statement was met with more and more laughter including me and my partner. One thing was for sure: After that, I rarely hear jokes about my size.

Everyone I work with has found out about me being gay. I tried to keep it within close-knit circles, but that's like trying to keep a tiger in a dog kennel. I'm sure that people call me a fag and make fun of me behind my back. It doesn't bother me because those same people would still make fun of me for something else if I was straight. Cops make fun of everyone for something. If they talk too much on the radio, we make fun of them. If they crash a car, we make fun of them. If they get beat up, we make fun of them. It just is. Everyone is bound to be made fun of for something.

If there is anyone who has a genuine problem with my sexuality, it is usually the old-timers, and they are so scared to say anything that they keep their distance. In today's police departments, racism and politically incorrect discrimination isn't tolerated (good-natured jokes notwithstanding, of course). Getting an internal case filed for that is potentially career ending and nobody wants any part of it.

Even though everyone gets made fun of for something, it's even more so for a gay officer. We are also burdened with having to prove we are capable of doing the job. It's one thing to get to know people, become friends with them, and then tell them you're gay.

Even people who don't know any gay people say, "Well you're my friend and we've been through a lot together, so I don't care who you sleep with."

The problem, as I alluded to, is that once people start to find out about something like that, it becomes hot gossip. It becomes harder to get to know people and become friends with them, if they know about me and are adverse to gays. They are more distant and less willing to get close to me. Some people wouldn't have a beer with me after work if it were going to be just the two of us. I wouldn't classify that as discrimination. I always know when people start to come around because they begin to ask questions about when I first knew I was gay, or if I'm seeing anyone. Curiosity is always a good sign, and I'm happy to answer any questions.

Whenever I started a new assignment, I would find myself chewing tobacco again. With the help of a therapist I determined it was one of the ways I tried to overcompensate for being gay. Certainly a little sissy gay guy wouldn't chew tobacco. I could be tough, see? For some reason I believed that helped.

Discussing my sexuality is wholly relevant to my perspective. If I am to persuade anyone about this line of work, it's important to share my personal perspectives, which are influenced by me being gay.

On the job, my mentor was another cop who had been on for twenty years longer than me. We met my first night on special assignment, New Year's Eve 1999. I hadn't graduated from the academy yet, but the city feared the apocalypse, and even the recruits were given a post inside one of the government facilities. It was a boring night, and nobody wanted to talk to me except a man who I would soon look up to.

He guided me through the difficult times and was there with a listening ear or advice. I knew about six openly gay male cops working in the Denver Police Department. I worked the street with one other gay guy who was made fun of a lot—normal, I thought, because I figured all gay cops were destined to be made fun of forever. As time went on, I realized that my mentor, my newfound friend, was an exception—he was gay too, and people respected him. I wondered why this was. Then I realized the other cop I worked with was made fun of because he was kind of a goof, and would be the butt of jokes regardless of his sexuality. My friend, however, was well respected throughout the department, and I never heard a cross word about him. He introduced me to some other gay men who were also well respected. They all had one thing in common: they proved themselves capable of doing the job in various ways.

Many years before I was hired, my friend and his police partner were sitting at lunch when they saw a stickup in progress. They both chased the robber, and his partner rushed ahead. My friend rounded a fence and saw that the robber had shot his partner in the head and was running away.

With his dead partner at his feet, my friend returned fire and killed the robber on the spot. To avenge a cop killer shows everyone that you have what it takes to stop the most serious of criminals from harming other cops and the city. In the big picture, this was the end-all-be-all of things to do. It was the ultimate test, and he passed. I have often said that my friend could have showed up at work in a dress and high heels after that. I bet even the same disgruntled old-timers who don't like me would take one look at him and say, "Hey brother. What's new?"

The biggest misnomer about being homosexual is people think that just because a man is gay, he wants to sleep with anyone who has a penis. I always hear straight macho men say things like, "If I was in a locker room and one of those gays came in and looked at me, I'd kick his ass." Coincidentally, these are usually the same men who are the ugliest, yet believe they are the epitome of desire. Here's a good rule of thumb: If women don't like you, men won't either. These men can take their hairy backs, beer bellies, and balding heads, and prance around a gay locker room all day long, and the most attention any gay man would give them is to throw a towel at them so they'll cover up.

The younger cops I've worked with in my time on the job have all been good to me. They are curious, ask questions, and take an interest in me and my life—it's refreshing. Along with that, however, comes ridicule. I was sitting in the office with my team one day and they were all bicycle trained. (You have to go to some stupid class to learn how to ride a bike because apparently police ride differently than other people. This, of course, is really to limit the department's liability.) They were asking me if I was going to get trained. Now there are two things for certain. First, I don't like riding bicycles. Secondly, I didn't join the force so I could wear spandex and a dorky helmet and ride around on a bicycle all day. I want to be in a big intimidating police car that has a radio, air conditioning, drives fast, and has lights and a siren.

I explained to my team that it would be a cold day in hell before I was riding around on a bicycle. Then I threw in that nobody would want to see my chicken legs anyway, just for good measure, to assure no one would beat me to the punch. Apparently, I took the wrong angle, thinking they would make fun of my legs because another cop said, "If we took the seat off would you do it?" To this day, that was probably one of the fastest, best lines I have ever heard anyone come up with, and I laughed hysterically along with them. (And by the way, the answer is still "No.")

The next time you come across a gruff cop, it may just be his thick skin you're observing. Rest assured we still have feelings. Besides keeping our emotions in check, this callousness also benefits officers by protecting us against all the horrific things we have and will see.

6
HOLLYWOOD HOMICIDE

Everyone wonders what it will be like to see their first dead body. I wasn't sure how I would handle it. I thought for sure it would be a while before I'd have to cross that bridge. But I was wrong. It couldn't have been an elderly person in a nursing home who went peacefully in their sleep. Instead, it had to be a depressed, lonely, upper-middle-aged man who went out to the cemetery and blew his head off with a double-barrel shotgun while visiting his wife's grave.

When we got there, his body was sitting under the tree he had leaned up against. Every part of him looked fine except for the spot in the middle of his face where his head had split apart in a straight line. Where his brain should have been was just an empty cavity. I wondered where his brain was, but my question was quickly answered when I saw most of it lying in a pile a few feet away.

I was surprised at my reaction. The whole scene looked fake. It looked as if a Hollywood makeup artist had bloodied up a doll and set it up to look like a dead body. I tried not to stare at it, but there was a powerful curiosity that held my attention, granted in small doses (my stomach was weaker than my mind).

I wondered if we as a society have been so desensitized by Hollywood that movies looked real and real life looked fake. I still don't know the answer to that. Thoughts about how much pain this man must have been in, and the fact that his family now will have to grieve the loss of a second parent started to enter my mind, but I quickly put a stop to it. I was better off not knowing. What's done was done, and all we could do was make sure nobody had killed him and made it look like a suicide, and then clean up the mess.

I've seen several dead bodies, and have become desensitized to them, much like every other cop on the force. It's not uncommon after some time on the job to be standing over a dead person inquiring as to where everyone wants to eat dinner. Cops have to be like this because with death so ubiquitous, we can't think about the family and friends who just lost a loved one. We can't think about the aftermath, the pain and trauma that's going to take families and friends years to recover. If we did, after a while, we couldn't function. The sheer grief would be debilitating. Distracting ourselves from what we are seeing is the only way to keep going.

Thankfully, death scenes don't bother me as much as I would have anticipated—I'm sure this is actually a protection mechanism. The guts and the gore don't usually get to me, but sometimes it's not the shootings and stabbings that are the nastiest. Oftentimes it's the less intense injuries, like broken bones. I hate the sight of a broken bone. An arm just dangles in a "U" shape, or it shrinks to half size. It's one of those bizarre things that's difficult to look at for any period of time. Of course if this broken bone involves a compound fracture, especially of the femur, it will undoubtedly be extra nasty. I have seen a handful of them in my life and I know I will never get used to them, but at least I don't shout, "Oh my God" anymore when I see one.

I first saw a compound fracture of the leg in a drunk driving accident. The cars were so mangled it reminded me of a class I took once as punishment for a speeding ticket. Most of us have taken the "Alive at 25" program where, in order to get a speeding ticket reduced, students are forced to sit through hours of pictures, stories, and movies. They show bent-up pieces of metal that are vaguely reminiscent of a car. For four hours after the class, you drive like your life depends on it. Then, before you know it, you're lip-syncing to Ariana Grande, eating a cheeseburger, and driving with one knee.

The Ford Probe that had hit a light pole at ninety miles an hour was mangled just like in the photos I'd seen in class. The driver, a drunk, was alive, walking around and talking. The front passenger, dead on the spot, was lying in the road a little ways away from the car with a sheet covering him. The fireman had done this to give some dignity to the man and to try to reduce the number of rubberneckers creeping by. That guy was the kind of dead where you look at him and go, "You know he's dead."

The rear passenger was in the back of the ambulance. I went to talk to the guy about what had happened in the accident. When I opened the ambulance door I should have seen the bottom of two feet staring back at me. Instead I saw the bottom of a left foot facing me, but it was paired with the front shin of his right leg. The top half of the leg was fine and intact. A few inches above the knee was where things went south. A femur bone with jagged edges was sticking out of the middle of the thigh and the rest of his leg was at an angle you wouldn't think possible. The muscle and surrounding tissue stopped, but the bone kept going for a bit until it ended at serrated edges.

One of the worst things anyone can do when someone is injured is to tell them that it's bad. Even if someone is shot fifteen times and still talking, they are supposed to be told, "Oh, it's nothing. It's minor. You'll be fine." If someone—especially a cop, firefighter, or paramedic—takes one look and says, "Holy shit! You're fucked!" it only sends them into panic. The mind is a powerful thing. If a person thinks they're dead, they will probably crash, but if they think it's possible to survive, their chances are better.

I took one look at this leg and accidentally screamed a slur of swear words together that to this day, I'm not sure what I said or if it made any sense. The one general meaning of my expletives was obvious: "You're fucked."

I never did find out if this guy lived or died. I'm almost glad I don't know because if I ever got a compound fracture, the first thing I would think of would be that poor soul lying on the stretcher screaming in pain.

Whether or not the desensitization of gore is the brain's protection mechanism, most dead bodies just lie there while the topic of conversation above is if anyone caught the season finale of *Game of Thrones*.

However, there's an exception to every rule. One type of dead body, no matter if it's a natural death or a homicide, really gets to me, and that's the body of a dead infant.

Thankfully, there aren't too many days in one's life which are cursed enough to have to see two dead infants.

It is precisely such a day that can call into question one's choice of vocation. I've come to find there aren't many things on this job to which I have not built up some sort of immunity. Dead people, family violence, shootings, stabbings, robberies, assaults, and so on—all become "normal" in daily life. Cops come to investigate them, not associate with them. Each call is just another experience. Experience, to me, means taking tidbits here and there in the form of a "memo-to-self" where I learn how not to fall prey to a similar situation. But babies and dogs have come to be my Achilles Heel.

The first infant death was heartbreaking. He had suffered from a disease and the death, while tragic, was expected. The difficult part was to see a dead infant lying there, perfectly still. The poor boy was wearing only a diaper, and all that could be seen was a little white of his eyes. A tiny bit of saliva had bubbled out of the corners of the mouth and the mother continued to sit over him, cradling him while sobbing uncontrollably. She held him and rocked him as if her comfort would bring him back to life, but his color was off. It was the color of skin that was obvious life had left the body. What was even harder was that the woman's other child had succumbed to the same fate a couple of years prior at the age of three.

As the coroner did his investigation, I stood by as more and more family members began to arrive. I soon noticed a large man with a blank white security badge standing over the mother. It's the type of card workers wear on a long cord around the neck to gain entry to their workplaces. I hadn't seen this guy around the house yet. Then I figured he probably wasn't a family member since he was holding a notepad and a pencil, which was perched to attack the paper at any moment. I looked him up and down and he introduced himself as a reporter from the local paper.

"And you just came in the house?" I stuttered in disbelief. He informed me that quite to the contrary, he was invited to enter. After I told him to get out of the house, he stood out on the sidewalk and paced impatiently back and forth. When the coroner and I finally left, he asked, "What did the baby die from?" In one of my favorite lines, the coroner replied, "It died from none of your business, that's what."

Well, thankfully that's over, I said to myself as I drove away from the house. I didn't make it very far when I received a call to assist the ambulance on a ten-month-old who was not breathing. When I arrived, the ambulance must have beaten me only by a few moments, and two firefighters were rushing out of the house. One of them held a limp baby girl as the other was doing chest compressions with two fingers. When they got the baby in the ambulance, they laid her on the gurney, and I noticed a familiar color in her legs. It was a color I don't have a name for, a color that was a little off.

The firefighters and one paramedic were in the back of the ambulance. Normally, I would ride down in the ambulance with the child but there wasn't room, so I followed behind in my car instead. When we all got to the emergency room, a swarm of people began poking the baby, taking blood, x-rays, and other vitals. They were massaging the chest and sticking tubes down the throat of this limp little girl.

I wasn't aware of this until that day, but the employees of this hospital were known for their disdain for cops. One of the nurses looked at me and then pulled the curtain just far enough to block my view. It was probably for the best.

The doctor finally called off the effort and pronounced the infant's death. I turned around just as a frazzled nurse came up to me; she told me, "I was talking to the father and trying to find out what happened so we could help the baby. He told me that he left the child alone with his wife [the stepmother]."

"Uh-huh." I encouraged what I knew wasn't going to be something I wanted to hear. She continued on about how the father had made the stepmother wait in the car in the parking lot of the hospital. When the nurse inquired as to why, he said, "Here, you talk to her," as he thrust his cell phone at her. What I heard next almost made me throw up. The stepmother told the nurse that she had put a pillow over the baby's face to stop her from crying.

As if that weren't haunting enough, the worst part was the drive down to police headquarters with the wicked stepmother handcuffed in my back seat. She asked all about my life. She wanted to know where I grew up, went to high school, how old I was, if I was married, and if I had kids of my own. She talked about the weather and her baby. Not the one lying lifeless in the hospital, but the one in her womb, which was about six weeks away from being born.

She was chipper and upbeat, smiling and giggling as if we were newfound friends. She didn't cry. She didn't ask what was going to happen next. She only asked once if I could tell her if anything had happened to the baby, but in a tone that one would expect from someone who was talking about their hobbies.

We hadn't told her the baby had died, only that the hospital staff was still working. Homicide detectives wanted to break the news to her on camera and not give her time to think of a cover-up story. I didn't get to hear the interview or find out whatever came of this woman. To be completely honest, I was so mortified by her lack of concern, I didn't want to take the chance of going to court and finding out she wouldn't receive any jail time. I don't know if she did or not.

Some people die and have no friends to notice they are missing. They may not speak to their relatives, if they even have any. If they do, the family probably lives far away. Some of them die and are found shortly after. Unfortunately, others die and aren't discovered until the smell is running neighbors out of their homes.

On this next call it was the latter, and what made it even more complicated was the deceased woman's hoarding disorder. The smell of decomposition was strong when we met the out-of-town brother on the front porch of the house. He had finally decided something must be wrong and flew into town to check on his sister. We got the key from the landlord and tried to assure the brother everything was fine, but judging by the smell on the front porch, not only was everything *not* alright, but it also wasn't going to be pretty.

When we went into the house, we saw it was stacked floor to ceiling with everything one could imagine. Coffee cans, magazines, newspapers, trash, boxes, and other arbitrary belongings were everywhere. There were small paths carved out. One path was from the door to a recliner chair in the living room, the only seat available in the place. There was a television about four feet away on a pile of stuff, with another pile of stuff on top of it. There was stuff between the TV and the chair, but stacked low enough that the TV was still visible. Another path went into the kitchen. Then there was another path to the bedroom.

Ah, the bedroom. In there was a loft made out of two-by-fours with no lower bunk. The mattress was stacked almost all the way to the ceiling. There was a ladder up to the bed but I'm not sure how one would get from the top of the ladder onto the mattress without being able to levitate horizontally. Under the loft was more crap piled up to the bottom of the bed. The mattress was a black and white striped prison-looking mattress with no sheets on it, and on top of the mattress was a swollen, bloated, naked, stinky, dead woman.

Now as a smaller guy, I had trouble making it through the narrow paths on my way to the bedroom. It was like trekking through a rainforest while using a machete to hack away the branches. On the way back to the front door, it was like I was a Grand Prix driver hugging corners smoothly as I darted for fresh air. I'm sure that wasn't a reassuring sight, to see the cops come hurrying out of your sister's house, gasping for fresh air.

I informed the brother of the situation and sent him to the hotel while I waited for the coroner—outside, of course. When he arrived, I was forced into going back in the apartment with him. We went in and made it to the bedroom, all the while I was trying to use my shirt to mask the smell. This would prove to be little help. I climbed up on one of the lower support arms of the loft so that I could see the woman, and he did the same at the other end of the bed. We popped our heads up in between the narrow area between the woman's swollen stomach and the ceiling. I was at her head and he was— well, inadvertently right between her spread legs. His eyes naturally diverted to the first place anyone's would, and then he looked at it, looked at me, and said, "I'll never be the same again."

The problem would soon be discovered that this woman had been there so long she was actually stuck to the mattress. The gases had bloated her already large body into a gargantuan mass. One false move and she would pop, and that's no joke. There was no way to get her body through the narrow paths in the apartment, so the coroner decided we had to bring her body through the window, which was probably twelve feet off the sidewalk below.

The fire department was called. The hose draggers came and cut the bed up with a circular saw to get the mattress down to a workable level. Because she was stuck to the mattress, they decided to wrap her up like a taco. They then secured it with some rope around the outside of the mattress.

Next was the window problem. There was no way this human fajita wrap was making it through the window. They had to remove the frame and cut out a larger hole in the side of the house to make it work. The firemen then fastened two-by-fours to the bottom of the mattress so it could be carried like one would carry royalty on a platform above their heads.

When the firemen tried to bring her to the window, they had to hold the mattress high enough to clear all of the items piled below. That's when she started to drip dead body juices all over them. If it were me, I would have dropped my end of the contraption, run for a bath, and probably resigned, but they kept on going. They called for me to help, but I informed them they would have better chances of finding a nun to sleep with than getting me anywhere near that mattress.

They finally got her to the window ledge. By this time I had moved outside where I had front row seats for what happened next. They began easing her out of the window when I heard someone yell, "Oh shit! There she goes. Look out!"

The mattress began to tip and then she broke free. The next thing I saw was this naked balloon slip off the mattress and begin her descent to the concrete. The firemen and the coroner were running for their lives. The poor woman landed on her head with the weight of her body still above her. Her neck bent under her mass and the body folded over the top of her head. Just when I thought it was all over, the head was flung out from underneath the body, and I had to duck to avoid being hit by the teeth that had shot out of her mouth like a slingshot. There was dead silence for a few moments. Then something broke the silence.

"This is going to be tough to explain," the coroner mumbled. Then there was another momentary stretch of silence followed by an explosion of awkward laughter from everyone as we realized that this autopsy was now going to have to rely on our detailed documentation to make any sense of the unbelievable thing that had just happened. It sounds sick to laugh at, but it couldn't be helped. I don't think we really knew how to process what we had just witnessed, so nervous laughter prevailed.

7
WASH YOUR MOUTH OUT WITH SOAP

Cops have to be careful what they say. Sometimes I can be fully justified to say, "Sit the fuck down." There have been several instances where this applied, when I was alone with a hostile group of people. I had no control over the situation, nobody was listening, my safety was in jeopardy, so to get people to follow my order, I reverted to obscenities. This established a command presence and let people know I meant business. Most of the time it's very effective.

I believe all departments should still recognize and acknowledge there are situations where swearing is appropriate. It's important to realize the people we deal with can be dangerous. Situations can and do evolve quickly. Control can be lost in a matter of seconds.

Remember the inexperienced Georgia officer who was shot? Of course the word "fuck" may not have saved his life, but who knows what would've happened if the officer stood his ground and told the man, "Put the gun down or I'll put a bullet in between your fucking eyes!" What I *do* know is that this shouldn't be considered discourtesy.

There are a ton of people—typically in lower income, high unemployment, less educated areas—who incorporate swearing into their communication styles. Keep in mind, every race has people who fit into this category.

These folks are not insulted by the sound of swear words and don't say things like, "Oh my God, the cop just said 'fuck'!" They actually understand better when spoken to as they speak. If you say to someone in the ghetto, "Now ma'am, I'm sure you realize the potential dangers of smoking marijuana with your young children in the room, and I highly recommend you not continue that kind of behavior. I'm going to have to incarcerate you for this little incident for 'Wrongs to Minors,'" your meaning may not come across.

"What the fuck are yous talking about?" they would most definitely say.

On the other hand, if I said, "What the fuck are you doing? You can't smoke that shit with your kids around, what's wrong with you? Are you fucked in the head? You're going to jail for fucking up your kids!" they usually say, "Aw…shit."

At first, even I was surprised when people were not offended by foul language, but remember, for some people, this is how they talk; it's not offensive to them. They don't give it another thought.

There's a large group of people for whom foul language is offensive. It would not be such a hot idea to walk into a burglary victim's house in the wealthiest area and say, "What the fuck is wrong with you? You left your back door unlocked? Jesus Christ, what the fuck did you expect?"

To these people, hearing a cop swear is like hearing their child's kindergarten teacher drop an F-bomb in the middle of a Dr. Seuss book. To them, this language is surprising, shocking, and inappropriate. And while I agree this language is not appropriate in everyday normal citizen encounters, it happens. Most of the time it just carries over because officers spend a great deal of each day swearing with the regular clientele. I'm asking for a little leeway.

I once responded to a call of a family disturbance. When my cover officer and I arrived at the house, there was a fat, drunk, slob of a woman. She was about sixty years old, and was leaning out of a bedroom window screaming for help.

As we got closer, I thought that she probably was not hurt at all, but called so we could make a run to the liquor store for her. In a hoarse voice she screamed something that was surely indiscernible to everyone but a fellow drunkard. Her top was falling down and her right breast was sagging out. She didn't seem to mind much about her exposure. The house was a little run down but not in terrible shape. I asked what the problem was.

"That prick son of mine locked me in this room and I can't get out. This is my fucking house and I want out of here!" bellowed the woman.

I communicated the obvious solution first: "Ma'am, you're on the inside of the bedroom. Just open the door and wander into the house." I was proud of myself for this wit and thought how all those years of schooling really had paid off.

"I know that, for Christ's sake. He turned the door handle around and locked it from outside the room. I'm locked in here!" she screeched.

We attempted to knock on the front door to contact the son who had grounded his mother, but she interrupted us, slurring, "I told you already, he's asleep and stoned. He doesn't hear shit when he's high."

Eventually we were forced to climb in through the bedroom window. This was not as easy as it might sound. Naturally, there was a sharp, pokey evergreen bush outside the window which hadn't been trimmed since the Abraham Lincoln administration. It obstructed any easy path into the house. We were forced to make our way through and then over this bush to get to the bottom of the window. After extensive poking and prodding from the bush, and a few scrapes from the aluminum window frame, we made our way inside.

Luckily for us, the bedroom door was not installed on any edition of *This Old House* with Bob Vila, and with a little jimmy using a pocket-knife, we managed to pop the door open.

The son, as promised, was passed out on the couch with a marijuana bong and a baggie of weed next to him on the coffee table. The man I would have expected to find would have resembled a skater punk, about eighteen years old with new tattoos and body piercings everywhere, but instead we found a man in his early thirties sleeping in his jeans and Metallica T-shirt.

We woke him up. It took him a few seconds to speak because he had to pry his jaw open. The pot had made his saliva a thick substance, which permeated his entire mouth, especially the corners, effectively gluing it shut.

He finally greeted us with the same standard welcome I like to use when people come to my house: "What the fuck do you want?" After we had a long talk and a ticket for the pipe and weed, I explained to him that he wasn't allowed to lock his mother up in the bedroom no matter how irritating she was. "This is your mother's house after all, and you are living under her roof."

My entire talk to this man was punctuated by his mother standing behind us repeating me and adding a few expletives: "Yeah, did you hear that? This is my fucking house!"

I continued, ignoring her. "You can't lock your mom up in her room."

"Yeah asshole, you can't do that shit!" she slurred.

For some reason, during our little talk, I remember saying these exact words: "You're just going to have to find something else to do with your mother besides locking her in the bedroom."

About three weeks later I got to work and the details of a homicide were buzzing through the roll call room. I heard the address and thought, *That sounds familiar.* My partner came up to me and muttered, "Well, I guess he took your advice and found something else to do with his mother."

"W-w-what?" I gulped.

"He killed her, cut her up, and hid her body between the mattress and box spring. Nice going," he said smugly.

For sure his comment was aimed at thickening my skin. I know I didn't really say anything inappropriate nor could I have even fathomed the son's solution, but it really made me think about trying to be aware of what I'm saying to people at all times.

Now that's something I wish I hadn't said, but there are a few things I *have* said that I still laugh about to this day. There are a couple of different techniques used to get guilty people to come clean. Most people will lie, even if it's a terrible one, until they have been caught red-handed.

If the cops can't get them dead to rights, then sometimes *we* lie to *them*. This is a popular technique. Cops are famous for bluffing—you can use the term lying if you prefer. We can lie to people and deceive them to find out the truth. Those of you who think this isn't righteous or fair need to be slapped around with a wet glove. After all, it's criminals we are dealing with, not Boy Scouts. We have to fight fire with fire.

In my third year, I went to a phone harassment call at a bar. This was a cougar bar, the kind of bar where forty-some-year-old women go to try to get a new man, usually a younger one.

One of the female bartenders was upset because her ex-boyfriend was in town, had come to the bar, and drank too much. Naturally, he became obnoxious and began swearing, yelling, and causing a scene. The bouncers ended up having to physically throw him out. After leaving, he began repeatedly calling the bar to harass everyone.

He threatened the waitress and the staff and said he was going to come back and kill them all. The man called about every thirty seconds, and since the bar is a place of business, they couldn't exactly take the phone off the hook.

When I arrived there, I got the story from a few of the employees and the waitress. The man called four or five times within the first few minutes I was there. I even answered the phone once with the bar name to hear some of this for myself.

"Fuck you, you piece of shit. I'm gonna come down there and kick your ass. You're fucking dead, do you hear me?" But before I could respond, the line went dead. Moments later the phone rang again.

"Hello?" I said as if expecting to find my grandmother on the other end of the line.

"Eat shit, you fuck-knocker. Why don't you be a man and meet me out front so I can kick your fucking ass?"

Click. The dial tone again.

Between obscene calls, I filled out the warrant for the man's arrest for threats to injure a person, harassment by use of the telephone, and disturbing the peace.

"You're never going to arrest him," said the waitress. "He's only in town for the weekend and I have no idea where he's staying. He's leaving on Monday to go back to California."

Surely this man shouldn't be allowed to get away with this, I thought. If he got back to California without being arrested and didn't return for a year, he would most likely never have to answer these charges. Warrants for city charges of this minor nature are only active for one year.

I thought of how to lure the man to me, and that's when it struck me. Just then, the phone rang again. I answered it, calling out his name and introducing myself as a police officer.

"Bullshit. This ain't the police. You're just saying that to scare me," he slurred.

I knew I had to find a way to prove I was the police and get my idea out before he got scared, hung up, and never called back.

"Look, I'm with the police and I gotta tell you something," I said. "I hate this bar. I've been trying to close this bar down for a year now, and I never have enough to do it. The bouncers are dicks and they're always abusing people and violating their rights." I heard him start to agree about how his rights had been violated, but I continued, "To tell you the truth, sir, I've only been here about ten minutes and I already hate your ex-girlfriend."

"Yup, that's what I've been trying to tell you!" he said. I wondered how he had been trying to tell me anything in the midst of all his swearing, cursing, and threatening, but didn't stop and analyze that.

"I can close this bar down," I continued, "but I'm going to need you to sign a complaint for the brutality the bouncers perpetrated on you and write a statement for me. I can probably even give your ex a ticket for instigating the whole thing." I tried to use big legal-sounding terms to sound convincing.

"But how do I know you're really a police officer? What if you're just trying to trick me?" he questioned.

"Well, it's real easy," I told him. "You hang up and call 9-1-1 and you ask them if I'm an officer, and make sure you're really talking to me. When you're convinced, give me a call back because I need to talk to you some more," I explained. I gave him my last name.

The man did indeed call and was assured I was a police officer. I was sitting there as nervous as the first time I had to speak in front of an audience. I had come to find out in police work that it's rare to get justice. Most crimes go unsolved. We show up, take a report, and try to reassure the victim to make them feel safe again. It's not often that we get to catch the bad guy and make the arrest ourselves. This was my chance to take the report and make the arrest, and my anxiety was brewing up my esophagus and into the back of my throat. Then, the phone rang.

"Hello," I answered, hoping it wasn't some drunken patron wondering if they had left their credit card at the bar.

"Hey, it's me" came the voice from the other end. "You're serious about this? You want to close down this bar?" the man asked.

"Yes I do. I hate this bar and I hate the people that work here."

He agreed to meet me at the nearest highway off-ramp. I went there and waited for him. I had another officer meet me there in case he decided to fight. We waited and waited and he didn't show. I knew this was too good to be true. The man was probably too scared to meet us and decided to pass out in his hotel room. He would go back to California and never pay for what he did.

It was at this point that a car crept forward toward us, revealing the driver's uneasiness. Then the man exited the vehicle and identified himself. I walked over to him, thanked him for coming to meet me, and when I shook his hand, I twisted it behind his back and put him in handcuffs. I told him he was under arrest and listed out the charges. I put him in the back seat of my car and as I put the car in drive, he said only one sentence to me: "That's really fucked up."

Lies on behalf of the police certainly lead to arrests, but instances like the last one are rare. Another more common example of cops lying is when we tell someone we got their fingerprints or other evidence even if we didn't. They end up confessing, figuring they've been busted.

Confessions are how most of the crimes are solved today. Unfortunately for most of you, sometimes people who are innocent get lied to as well, but in the end you have nothing to hide. I guess that's just the way it works. The innocent people come away with a bad taste in their mouth, and usually wonder what they did to deserve the third degree.

Unfortunately, cops are not human lie detectors. If criminals are to be caught, a few people who aren't guilty will have to endure unnecessary scrutiny and lies. Ideally, society would understand this is for the greater good.

Most people will never be in a situation where this is the case, however. It's doubtful anyone would get the third degree when stopped for speeding. Sometimes good people are in the wrong place at the wrong time. Those are the instances I ask for a little more patience and understanding.

The second technique utilized by law enforcement is threatening. Sometimes it is a legitimate threat like, "You will go to jail if you don't do what you're told." Other times it's a threat that cannot be carried out. Once in a great while a threat is a little extreme. What's more important—getting felons off the street or being perfect gentlemen cops? Everyone knows the answer to that.

About five years in, I found myself in the projects with the highest crime rate in Colorado. I was driving around when I ran the plate of a car whose occupants all looked at me like they had just seen a ghost—first clue that something was wrong. The young male driver looked like he should be presenting a turtle at show-and-tell, not driving a car. Something was definitely up.

The plate came back stolen, and by the time I got turned around, car doors were flying open and the four kids were running away. I called out the foot chase as we dashed through the apartments, dodging the metal wires between green belts adjoining the different buildings. This metal wire is supposed to be a clothesline, but it is very hard to see at night and serves as a decapitator if hit full-steam-ahead.

Three of these little turds stuck together and the fourth went on his own. Among the three was the driver, my primary target. The three ran into a corner, where they all skidded to a stop and turned to face me. I wasn't too far behind them. I had my gun pointed at them as I was trying to yell at them to stop and talk into the radio simultaneously. It's important to keep everyone apprised of my location as the chase progresses. There have been a few occasions where I'm yelling my location into the radio, and then forget to let go of the transmit button and scream, "Come back here you little fuckers!" Thankfully, this wasn't one of those times.

The kids looked around for an escape route and found one to the south. Just as they were launching on this new path, ignoring my commands to stop running, an idea came to me.

I came to a halt. I took aim, and calmly and in my best Al Pacino "Say hello to my little friend" voice and with a little crazy eye, said, "Say goodnight you bitches!"

All three of them dropped, lying prone on the ground with their hands in front of them as if they were citizen volunteers at the academy during arrest control training.

Of course I couldn't have shot them, nor would I have ever premeditated such a statement—it just came out. It was a powerful hollow threat that worked, and three car thieves were behind bars because of it. The community was safer not having three felons do God knows what as they tried to elude the pursuing police. Where cops get into trouble with lying, bluffing, or just the overall third degree is when we get used to doing this and forget it isn't warranted in every situation. Most people in the world are good, hard-working, honest people. The majority of people in this country will only have contact with law enforcement a few times in their lifetime. It could be a car accident, a theft, or a burglary, but usually they are the victim, not the suspect. Even if you've had more than one of these things happen to you, most likely it was years between incidents. Most people don't have to deal with us over and over again within a short period of time.

Police deal with the same small sect of society repeatedly. We respond to calls involving the same houses, the same people, the same problems over and over again. I call them our main clientele.

If cops are going to deter criminal behavior, sometimes that means not always being nice. Sometimes we are empathetic, sometimes we are mean, and sometimes we lie. Different situations call for different techniques. Language has to be a tool applied with a broad brush.

If they are breaking the law or endangering themselves or others, language has to be used in a way that has the highest probability of success. Although swearing, lying, and threatening people is probably not the preferred method for handling things, it usually has the highest success rate. These things, sometimes combined with a little crazy eye, saves lives.

8
I'M TELLING DADDY!

There are a lot of different types of snobs in this world. All of them are irritating, not just to cops, but to everyone. These are the people who have no concept of the real world. They believe they're at the center of the universe, and that the law does not apply to them. Everyone knows a snob when they see one, and they are as ridiculous to me as they are to you.

Police officers can park wherever they want. When I would park to check an alarm and someone tells me, "It must be nice to just park on the curb," I say, "It would be if I was going shopping, but unfortunately I'm checking an alarm at this business." If something happens and cars have to race in to save my life, my car will be a big sign where I am. What if I start checking this business and someone starts shooting? I want my car nearby so I can hide behind it while the bullets are flying at me. That's not what the public sees. They see a lazy cop parking on a sidewalk because he doesn't want to walk.

I would explain to people that it's necessary for me to be close to my car in case anything happens. The difference between life and death could be the time it takes to run to a legally parked car three blocks away. A robbery call could come out, an officer could call for help at any second, and I need to be as close to my car as possible.

I would tell these people, "If your daughter was being beaten by her husband, would you want me to run to my car all the way down at the next block or have it right here so I could get there faster and help her?" They would agree.

Going through this explanation day after day and time after time, it wasn't long before I was having a bad day and just started saying, "Mind your own business." If I could hold a class and teach everyone at once why this happens, I would be pleasant and even entertain stupid questions at the end. Explaining to people one by one is undoubtedly futile, so I stopped. Nevertheless, it soon became department policy to park your car legally unless you were on a legitimate police action—that means no parking illegally when stopping in to grab coffee. Now I hope the extra time it takes to get to my car if something *were* to happen doesn't cost someone their life. Guess the snobs won that one.

Then there are the snobby *and* ignorant people who think because they watch *Law and Order*, they are world-class attorneys. These are the people who tell you, "You can't do that! I know my rights." They say things like, "You can't come in without a warrant."

Without getting into a constitutional lesson, there are several exceptions to a warrant. There are instances where we are not getting a warrant, not required to get one, nor do we even have to ask to come into your house. We are coming in, end of story.

If neighbors call and say they heard a man and woman fighting in the house next door, when we get there, we are coming in to make sure there isn't anyone lying in a bedroom bleeding, beat up, or dead. If, for instance, a husband had beat his wife almost to death and she was in the bedroom clinging to life, do you think he would tell the police this when he answered the door? If these circumstances exist, the police are coming in to check.

If the cops came to your door and told you they had a call of a fight at your house, most people would say, "Everything's fine here. You can come in and take a look if you want." These are the normal, rational people. It's the indignant cop haters and people who are up to no good who tell the cops to go away.

Cops can be our own worst enemy. I always tried to explain why and what I was doing while on a call. A perfect example of this is when I was on a call of a family disturbance. Tempers were flaring and everyone was yelling at each other. The first thing was to make sure nobody has any weapons on them. The second thing was to sit them down and restrict their movement so they can be seen and their movement controlled.

If someone is going to be sat on a couch, it's common to check under and around the cushions to make sure there is nothing that can be used as a weapon. But start looking under someone's cushions without saying anything and they get angry. I always explained, "Everyone is going to sit down until we get this figured out, and I'm going to make sure there aren't any guns or knives under these cushions before you sit here." People then usually acquiesce.

Oftentimes I think my badge should read, "Parenting Police" or "Marriage Counseling Police" or "Parents for Adults Police." Parents are scared today to discipline their kids. Nowadays after a spanking, the next step for the child is to call the police. While wearing the "Parenting Police" badge, cops must now intervene.

I would commonly hear: "Officer, my mommy just spanked me" or "Officer, tell that son of mine to clean his room or he's going with you!" These are seriously things that go on all the time. Grown adults call us and tattle on their children, and the children call us to tattle on their parents.

The people that call us to parent their kids don't seem to understand they are the ones who have the power. It isn't, nor should it be, the job of the local police to come to a house and tell a kid to clean his room or stop talking back to Mom or Dad. If I had my way, there would be a fine for calling the police unnecessarily. That's when I would say, "There isn't anything I can do for you, but here's a ticket for wasting my time."

Other times the badge should read "Marriage Counseling Police." I often hear voices in my head like, "Now, Mrs. Smith, you and your husband have been together for thirty years and you know how he is after work on Fridays. He likes to relax and watch television. This is not the time to start in on him about the dishwasher he hasn't fixed."

And, "Mr. Smith, how do you expect Mrs. Smith to keep this house clean for you so it's nice when you get home from work if her appliances aren't working? After all, she has asked you several times to fix the dishwasher. Can't you just look at it for a few minutes? Maybe it's something simple. After all, you've seen this episode of

Seinfeld a hundred times already and it's not even a good one."

It isn't the job of the police to get a spouse to behave. All of us have problems in our relationships. Most of us know there isn't anything the cops can do for us, and we don't call. A small percentage of people expect the police to wave a wand and fix everything. I tell people, "I'm sorry things aren't like a fairytale for you, but join the club. You think you're the only couple that fights?" I spend a lot of time wondering, *Just how is it I'm supposed to make your husband a better man?* If I had the answer to that, I wouldn't be a police officer, I would have a daytime talk show after *Dr. Phil.*

I also spend a good amount of time lecturing grown people on what I think they should have learned long ago in the socialization process. This is the role of "Parents for Adults Police." Lecturing works sometimes, and other times people could care less if they were being given the secret to eternal happiness. It was difficult to learn how to give lectures, especially when I was a young cop in my early twenties and the lecturee was old enough to be my father.

The first time I pulled somebody like this over and decided to lecture him (we're taught either a lecture or a ticket, but not both), it was awful. I was so nervous, my hands were shaking. I pictured having to scold my father, "Now I shouldn't have to explain to you about right and wrong. You know better. If I ever catch you doing this kind of thing again, you'll regret it. Do you hear me, buster? Look at me when I'm talking to you!" It just didn't feel right.

Instead I managed a weak and feeble, "If you wouldn't mind, sir, try not to do that anymore, sir."

After a while, I came to realize that most of the people cops deal with on a daily basis are not the more upstanding, productive members of society. These so-called adults are far less mature than I am even if they are twenty years older, and what they need is a good ass-chewing because they never got it from their parents. Eventually, it gets easier.

Police are sent to a situation and the goal is always to resolve the conflict. However, we can't spend weeks and months dedicating hourly counseling sessions to cure their deepest, darkest childhood issues. Instead, there are only five or ten minutes to help them, and then it's time to move on. When cops go on a call, just like a parent would do, we make a decision and it's final. Sometimes we put people in time-out (jail). Sometimes we take their allowance away (fine). But all the time, we have to figure out an immediate decision.

Cops develop a sense as to what will work. If an officer is talented, he or she can even tell what kind of demeanor will help. Should it be tough love? Is gentle and sensitive the way to go? Is this a time to be scary and intimidating?

Scaring somebody is a common tactic and usually an effective one. Unfortunately, a few police officers lose sight of their other options and end up resorting to this scare tactic every time. These are the cops that pull people over for minor traffic violations and say something like, "Do you know what I can do to you for this? I can haul your car away and throw your butt in jail. You'd probably have to do a couple of months in county. They'd like you in there, pretty boy."

To this, most decent, respectable people reply, "Gosh officer, I didn't realize the penalty for U-turns had gotten so stiff. I'm really sorry!"

These cops aren't bad people. Just like everyone else, they want to go out and make a difference. If you get pulled over by one of these more zealous officers and get the third degree for something petty, take some solace in the fact they are trying to make your neighborhood as safe as possible, even if they are a bit overboard.

When making a traffic stop, we were taught to decide whether or not to issue a ticket before getting out of the patrol car. In my department, we were not supposed to give "attitude tickets." Not all departments have this philosophy, and unfortunately, in my opinion, ours had it all wrong. The department grants and encourages officers' discretion, yet also expects us to decide if someone is going to get a ticket before even speaking with them. I'm not sure that's possible. Discretion shouldn't be based on a guess as to how someone is going to react.

I tested for another police department in my college town my senior year. I eventually bowed out of the testing process to work in a bigger city. During the oral interview, I was asked if I would give my mom a ticket. Of course there is no way I am going to write my mom a ticket—well, at least not on a normal day—but that wasn't what I told them.

Instead, I explained that she would have to pay the piper just like everyone else, and so I would write her a ticket. Then one of the interviewers tried to lead me down a path to help me change my mind. He asked, "What if your mom was especially upset because she had embarrassed her policeman son, and you could tell by talking to her that she would never do this again? What if she was very remorseful, and you could tell she had learned her lesson? After all, the goal of stopping someone is to correct their behavior, isn't it?"

I hesitated, but knew he was right and said, "Yes."

He continued, "Don't you think for some people, just being pulled over will stop their behavior and others might need something else to make them think twice?" Again, I agreed—after all, what choice did I have?

"So you wouldn't write your mom a ticket under those circumstances, would you?" he said encouragingly.

Now I was sure of myself. "Of course not!"

That department had it right. Under my department's philosophy, if my mind is supposed to be made up before the initial contact with a person, how am I supposed to know it's my mother before getting out of the car? In my mind, it's impossible to assess what means of enforcement is to be used before even talking to a person.

About two years in, I was almost done with my graveyard shift when a car ran a red light and almost struck several other vehicles going the other way.

I pulled the car over and as I walked up to the window I started, "Good morn—"

"I am late for a flight and I have a very important interview in Oregon and *you* are messing it all up!" came an angry voice from inside the car.

I was really and truly shocked, so I fired back, "Well you're not going to make it to the airport if you keep driving like that." I was proud of myself for such a witty comeback on short notice.

"I don't have time for this," the driver said. "I've gotta get going or I'll miss my flight." She began to put the car in drive to leave.

"If you drive off, you won't make it to Oregon until you get out of jail. Now give me your license, registration, and proof of insurance." I meant business now.

"I didn't even do anything!" she protested.

"You ran the red light back there," I snapped.

"That light was orange," she said.

That's always one of my favorite defenses. First of all, there is no orange light on a traffic signal. Secondly, the color orange is made from yellow and red, so if you *did* in fact see orange, it would have to have come from the red light being illuminated and then mixing with the yellow, which was no longer lit. It's as if people think there's one big light on a traffic signal, and similar to the speed lava rises in one of those lamps, the colors slowly fade into each other.

"I need your license, registration, and insurance then I'll get you out of here as quickly as I can," I said coolly, proud of my patience.

"Is this still your current address?" I needed the correct one to put on the ticket.

"No," she snapped.

"What's your current address?"

"I don't know. Just hurry up."

"Well how long have you lived there?"

"About six months."

"How could you not know your address if you've lived there for six months?"

"We don't have time for this and it doesn't matter where I live."

"I need your current address, ma'am." My patience was wearing thin. She finally gave me her address.

I had just got seated in the police car when she got out of her vehicle and started to walk back to me. This is a no-no for a couple of reasons. It's an officer safety issue to have someone approaching your car who you have not searched for weapons and don't know their intentions. Not to mention, it's also incredibly dangerous for her to be in the street walking around in traffic.

I got out and stood in the "V" made by my ajar police car door, and with as much authority as my 5'8" frame and 150 pounds could muster, I said, "Get back in your car. I'll be with you in a minute."

By this time, the thirty-one-year-old female, dressed elegantly in business attire obviously purchased especially for the day, now appeared to resemble Satan after you kicked him in the balls and stomped on his tail all while wearing a pair of pumps.

"You are ruining my life. I'm leaving. I have to go." She was now screaming and near hysterics, similar to if you had taken a bottle away from a two-year-old.

"You're the reason this is taking so long," I countered. "Now get back in your car before you go to jail." I really didn't want to take her to jail for disobedience to a lawful order, but at some point, the police have the right to win the conflict.

Finally, I raised my voice to signal that I was serious as a heart attack and yelled, "This is your last warning. Get in the car or you are going to be arrested." She did, but just as I got situated and picked up my pen to continue writing, here she came again. This time when she got out of the car she was on the cell phone.

"My father wants to speak to you." She held out her phone.

"I'm not going to talk to your dad, you're a grown woman."

"Oh yes you are." She pushed the cell phone into my ear.

I sighed. "Yes?" I said into the receiver.

"You are delaying my daughter's departure. She has a very important interview today," the man said, obviously attempting to sternly reason with me.

"No. *You* are now delaying your daughter's departure," I said.

As I began to hand the phone back I heard him say, "The light wasn't even red, it was orange."

As much as I wanted, I wasn't going to be able to let this go. I wondered if parental intuition extended to their offspring's driving habits.

"You aren't even here. How would you know?" I snapped as I grabbed the phone back. *Why am I arguing with this lady's father? This is ridiculous!* "Goodbye," I said into the phone and handed it back to her. "If you get out of that car again, you will go to jail." I promised myself this was the last time I would warn her.

She got back in the car. I finally got a chance to write the ticket and issued it to her. She ripped it out of my hands while I was trying to explain how she could either mail in the fine or appear in court if she wanted to fight it. Then she sped off as if the green flag had just been waved over the starting line at the Indianapolis 500.

I can't speak for all officers, but when I initially approached the car, if she would have said, "Oh my God, Officer. I'm so sorry. I have a big interview in Oregon today, I'm late for my flight, and I can't miss it. It's the most important interview of my life. I just want this job so badly. I should have gotten up earlier and now here I am driving like a madwoman running red lights and almost killing myself. I'll be more careful from now on, I promise," I would have turned away from the window and said, "Good luck with the interview." Truth be told, I probably would have settled for any part of that.

What would you do? Did this girl deserve a ticket? Would a warning have fixed the situation? That woman just didn't get it, and even with a ticket probably never will. But even so, maybe the fine and time off of work to go to court would be enough of a deterrent to stop her from doing that again.

Some people have a title wave of acid dumped in their stomachs the moment they are pulled over. These are the people that probably won't speed again for quite some time. For them, just being pulled over has them making deals with God. A ticket is going to really do nothing else for a person like this.

Most cops I work with in the patrol division—and this goes for me too—probably write tickets to about fifty percent of the cars we stop. The same doesn't apply for the traffic bureau. They write tickets all day as their primary function. Nevertheless, I'm sure when you get pulled over you hope it's one of us at the fifty percent level.

What if a cop pulls over another officer? Should they be issued tickets at the fifty percent level? People think the cops should be written every time, even if you agree that the general public should get breaks half the time. Most police departments will say officers should write other officers tickets, and that it isn't fair to put other cops above the law. I disagree with this. Consider your profession. If you work at McDonald's, you probably get free or discounted food. If you work for a mortgage industry, you get the company to eat the points on your loan or at least some of the fees. If you are a flight attendant or pilot, you and your immediate family get to fly for free. Why shouldn't cops get something?

Despite the double standard in this instance, being a police officer is still an amazing job. We may have to endure a few snobs now and then, but for the many people whose lives we change for the better, it's worth it. There's a certain look in someone's eye when that happens, and that's why I went to work every day.

9
STUPID IS AS STUPID DOES

Sometimes I wonder how stupid people made it this far in their life. How did they get dressed in the morning? How did they find their way out of their house? Did they remember to eat? How do they care for themselves? I'm not talking about people who don't know what year Columbus discovered America, I'm talking about a complete lack of common sense.

I saw a woman pushing a stroller with an infant in it. The woman was in the roadway, next to a perfectly good sidewalk, walking against the flow of traffic at night wearing all dark clothing. There were no reflectors on the stroller or the mother. What is wrong with people? There should be a law that says something to the effect of, "It shall be unlawful for any person to knowingly or unknowingly be an idiot." This law should be a felony and punishable by up to a lifetime of incarceration, at my discretion of course. This woman, instead of receiving the equivalent of a jaywalking ticket, would be locked up until such time as she can prove she's no longer stupid.

Officers are allowed to work off-duty—or as it's called in other places, moonlighting. This work is paid to you by the bar, bank, construction company, or other institution. The jobs are usually done in full uniform, and since police officers are police officers twenty-four hours a day, seven days a week, all the authority and arrest powers remain with us even when off-duty. It pays really well too, anywhere from $35 to $55 an hour.

Many cops say off-duty is one of the only reasons to do this job. It is regulated of course, and only twenty-four hours of this work is allowed each week on top of the standard forty-hour workweek. Off-duty bar stories could be a book unto themselves. When I'm working a regular patrol assignment and I respond to a bar on a call, people act differently than if I stand around the bar all night. When responding on a call, the police show up, have a mission, handle business, then leave. People usually are scared to approach and don't interfere.

"Oh shit. The cops are here," they say as they observe every move. Conversely, when working off-duty, it's like suddenly the police are transformed into the evening's entertainment. Our job then becomes to tell stories and answer questions about our personal life that we don't even share with a majority of our close friends let alone a complete stranger.

For the first couple hours, nobody usually says anything. They keep their distance but always seem to keep watch out of the corner of their eye to see where we are positioned and what is going on. As the night progresses, though, and their level of drunkenness becomes greater, they slowly get the courage to come up to talk and ask stupid questions.

While at a bar one night, this tall lanky guy came up to me and, as he touched my back, he inquired, "Is that a bulletproof vest you're wearing?" I told him yes and immediately he asked why something like this was needed at a bar, to which I promptly explained it might come in handy if I was shot. He refused to believe it was possible for me to be shot while working off-duty at a bar.

We then got into a lengthy discussion as to why it was necessary for me to have a gun while at a bar. He thought a Taser or some other weapon would have been more appropriate. After repeated attempts to explain, he failed to grasp the concept that police officers carry guns all the time, on or off duty. I told him of a recent time when two cops from my department were shot while working off duty at a private event. One of them was killed, the other wounded. It doesn't happen every day, but I'm not willing to take that chance. His only reply was, "Oh that wouldn't happen here."

When I first started working off-duty, I would entertain these barrages of questions from drunken patrons, but as the years wore on, my patience level decreased. It's not uncommon for a cop to tell people, "Go away." If I had a dollar for every time someone has asked, "Do you get paid for this?" or "Can I buy you a beer?" I wouldn't have to write this book. During my off-duty shifts, people came up every night and try to touch me, put their arms around me, or pinch my ass. To this day, I'm not sure why anyone would think any of that is a good idea. Even at my most drunk, I still would never think, *I've got it! I'll go pinch the cop's ass.*

I was sitting on a stool one night in the typical cop posture. There are a few of these postures cops are famous for, and I had them down pat long before being hired. One is to lean up against a wall and bend one leg at the knee. The sole of the bent foot goes up against the wall. This is the best posture to use when there is no place to sit down. It's a good idea to take turns with each foot to give a break to each side.

Another posture is to sit toward a corner of a table with one leg hanging down almost touching the floor. The other is a bit higher up. This posture says that the cop is ready to spring into action at any moment. If I was to sit all the way on the table and lean back, this would suggest I could be caught off guard.

On this night I was using the third type of posture, one associated with a bar stool. My legs were a bit spread, and my feet were fastened to the different crossbars at different levels of the stool so my knees were bent. One foot rests on the lower of the two crossbars, and the other goes around the side on the upper crossbar. Some woman came up to me, didn't say a word, backed her ass into my groin and began to give me a lap dance.

Two problems I saw with this: first, I'm gay. Second, I'm not at a strip bar waving money over my head in hopes of shoving it into a woman's underwear. When I pushed her away, she told me, "You're an asshole!"

Another night while working off-duty at a gay bar, I was standing near the entrance when a man approached me. I could tell he wanted to talk to me, so I looked away in hopes my lack of eye contact would give him a clue. (Lack of eye contact never works.)

As he got closer, he hunched over and continued to walk toward me. A moment later, his tongue was sticking out. By the time I figured out he was about to lick my badge it was almost too late. I gave him a shove backward and told him to go away. You would think this would be enough for an average person to apologize, but not this guy. He proceeded to tell me that he paid my salary and that he could do what he wanted because he was the one that actually owned my badge. I chose not to explain to him that the bar was the one paying me that particular night and that he owned no such thing. Instead I told him to go away. (That never works either.)

After several minutes of arguing with this guy, I told him that if he didn't go away he would be asked to leave. He told me that I didn't have the authority to throw him out. I gave him the usual warnings associated with this, which he laughed off, just like everything else I had told him.

Finally, I told him he was leaving. He didn't believe me. This argument went on for another couple of minutes until I told him that if he didn't leave, I would make him leave. This didn't work either. (Perhaps you're beginning to see how people bring on all this trouble by themselves.)

I tried to take him by the arm to escort him out, to which he ripped his arm away from me informing me at the top of his lungs, "You can't touch me!" This snowballed until I had good control of him and threw him out the front door. He turned around, finally having figured out this was not a game, and yelled at me, "You don't have to treat people like this just because they are gay!"

"*I'm* gay, you fucking idiot," I countered.

He stared at me for a second as if the last ripcord on his parachute had just been pulled and nothing happened.

"Oh," he said as he turned and walked away.

Other questions I get a lot are: "What's the scariest thing that's ever happened to you?", "What does it take to become a policeman?", "How much are you getting paid?", "What is all that on your belt?", "Do you like your job?", "Shouldn't you be out on the street instead of hanging out in a bar all night?", "Are you married?" "How do I get out of a ticket?", "What's your quota of tickets?", or "Do you stop only the nice cars?"

We are not at a job to be personal information booths. We are there to protect the public and the bar from criminal activity. We are not comedians, and it is not our responsibility to educate people on "the coolest thing we've ever seen." Once in a while, it's okay to entertain a few of these questions, just not night after night, week after week, year after year. However, the last two of these questions I would like to explain a bit, since they are questions a lot of people have.

During my time at the department, the patrol officers didn't have a quota of tickets. We could write twenty or none, it didn't matter. As far as the question about only stopping nice cars: No. We stop the ones that are speeding.

Not only are there those common questions we hear all the time (oh, I forgot the "Shouldn't you be eating a doughnut?" question), but there are other less common, but just as ridiculous ones. A girl once walked up to another officer and me while we were working at a bar. She asked us if we knew any magic. Without a thought, my partner said, "If I did, I would make you disappear." That still makes me laugh. Other ridiculous questions always deal with a person's "friend" and not the person asking.

Once a guy asked me, "If my friend was arrested for a DUI, is it common to tow their car even if there is someone else there to drive it?" This person was most certainly arrested for a DUI, obviously didn't think it was necessary for the police to tow his car, and now was secretly trying to find out if what the cop did was legitimate. Knowing a complaint hinged on my answer, I said, "Yup, everyone who gets a DUI gets their car towed."

After all of this badmouthing of the common public, I should mention that there are a few people who will say something like, "Thanks for being here." Or, "Thanks for doing a good job and protecting us." Those people don't go unnoticed and still give me a little assurance that there are some decent people out there. This only happens once or twice a night. The incidents with assholes occur about five times an hour. In four hours, that's approximately twenty times over the course of the shift. If there are around a thousand people in the bar, and if every time the idiot was a different person, only twenty out of the thousand would be assholes. This is a pretty small percentage.

However, if you were to go on a picnic at a beautiful park and put your blanket next to the outhouse, would you remember the pretty flowers or the shit smell? It's difficult to remember the few nice people when the negative incidents are twenty-to-two a night. If you work in a bar multiple nights a week as I did, that's even more difficult to keep focused on the good people and not the bad. Thanks to those of you who take the time to be the good ones.

One of the other types of people who are nice but irritating are the wannabe cops. They are usually security guards or bouncers, and think they've been deputized by the president. They will tell of their war stories as if the two of us had been partners for twenty years: "Then, the guy told me to bring it on. Well, I don't let anyone talk to me like that. I pulled out my baton and beat him senseless. Yeah, the cops came and told me what a good job I did. They took him to jail and he got twenty years."

I've found that these people are always "about to be hired" by some police force.

"Yup. I'm gonna get hired in January. I've got a couple DUIs in my background, and I was charged with statutory rape, but that was all bullshit and the judge took that off my record," he says. Yeah, sure he did.

I'll admit I'm hardly the poster boy for intimidation, but it never ceases to amaze me how often I get pushed, shoved, or punched at a bar. I once broke up a bar fight. I grabbed a guy from behind. Luckily, before this particular night, I had learned that when breaking up a fight, and especially when grabbing someone from behind to say, "Police department, just relax," the last thing I need is to be mistaken for a friend of the guy on the opposing side.

That night in particular, I grabbed the guy in a fight and gave him my standard line. I let him go and he turned around, looked at me, and took a swing at my head. I ducked and with my expandable baton, gained compliance (which is a fancy way of saying I hit him until he gave up). Maybe it's just me, but not in a million years, even at my most drunk and angry, would I ever turn around, see a cop who was trying to stop a fight, and decide that he needed to be taught a lesson for interfering. But I guess I'm one of the few, or so it seems.

I wish it were only off-duty that I came across stupid people, but that's hardly the case. Some of the people I feel sorry for because they are so stupid. I wish I could wave a wand and make their brains come alive, but in the end, it's hopeless. All people have to do is listen and do what they're told, but they don't, and once again, as you will see, they bring on their problems and misery all by themselves. To illustrate this, I've got one of my favorite stories.

The dispatcher called my car number and told me there was a burglary in progress. The neighbor calling saw a man break a side window to a house and crawl through the window. I got there first, and right behind me was a second car. I started to go around to the back, and on my way noticed the glass to a side window was smashed out and most of it was lying on the sidewalk. I relayed this information over the radio.

The other cop stayed in the front of the house. I went around to watch the back door. We weren't going to do anything until more cars arrived. I had my gun out and was crouched beside the corner of the house when I heard the back door open. A man started walking across the backyard with a handful of stuff from the house. He was holding some records and electronic equipment piled high in his hands. As authoritatively as I could I yelled, "Police department! Freeze!" just like they do on TV. Man, was I proud.

The man looked at me and ran back into the house. I must have sounded like Minnie Mouse, all high pitched and squealing, when I got back on the police radio and yelled, "He came out the back carrying stuff and he ran back inside." The dispatcher sounded an alert tone and asked for everyone to respond code 10. Then a K-9 officer got on the air and informed us he would be responding.

Lots of other people arrived, plus the K-9 unit. We announced several times and gave many verbal commands to give up and come out. Then the K-9 handler and his dog went to the side door and the handler yelled—as they always do—three times, "This is the police. Anyone in the house speak to me now or I'll release the dog and the dog will bite."

There was no response, and I was thankful the dog was going to be the brave one and go in after this guy. I mean, who knows where this guy was hiding, and if he had a gun, he would most certainly have had the drop on us. The dog went in the side door and the suspect jumped out from the end of the short hallway. The next thing I heard was screaming from the man and growling from the dog. The K-9 dogs can actually drag a full-sized man across a floor—who knew?

The dog pulled him out of the house and we handcuffed him. He had to go to the hospital for the dog bites and was charged with disobedience to a lawful order and resisting arrest.

Why wasn't he being charged with burglary, you ask? Well, that's simple. The house was his. His wife had locked him out after a major fight, leaving him stranded in his yard. He was angry with his wife, having been locked out, and I'm sure he thought, *I'll be damned if I let her keep my records!* So he broke the window and climbed in to get them, and the player of course.

My first thought was, *How bad does that suck? First he's locked out, then he has to break his own window and undoubtedly pay for it, gets bitten by a dog, has to go to the hospital, and then gets thrown in jail.* Then I thought, *Wait a minute. Had this guy done what he was told, he would have been handcuffed for a few minutes until we figured out what was going on and then let go.*

You may also be asking why it was we had to charge him with criminal charges. One might think, *The poor man's been through enough; can't you just take him to the hospital and let him go?* But thanks to our litigious society, if we did, and we were sued, there would certainly be questions from attorneys like, "Why did you have a dog bite my client? He obviously didn't do anything wrong since he wasn't arrested. Isn't it true you hurt an innocent man?" The truth is, we had to charge him to protect ourselves. Good thing we did. We were sued civilly, the city settled, but he didn't get much. He got less than he would have had we not charged him criminally.

City officials are also exhibiting stupidity in regard to deciding to settle frivolous lawsuits. It makes sense in the short term. Anyone can see it is cheaper to settle for $5,000 than spend $50,000 to litigate the case. However, what that does is encourage frivolity in litigation. A city is better off spending the extra money upfront to fight frivolous lawsuits because it discourages others. Years down the road, instead of handing out settlements to anyone who sues, the message would be sent that they don't tolerate these kinds of lawsuits.

Also, lawyers would be less willing to take on cases against a city that they know will fight them, especially if they think they might lose. And it shouldn't stop there. The city, after litigating a frivolous suit and winning, should turn around and sue the plaintiff. I'm sure this person could probably never make enough to reimburse the city for the legal fees, even after a lifetime of work. The city should see to it that their paychecks are garnished for the rest of their lives. Then we'll see how many people want to milk the city.

Instead, we settle, and people who are hit by felons stealing cars sue the city because the police "shouldn't have been chasing them." They know they'll never get a dime out of the crook, so they go after the deep pockets. As a result, we are not allowed to chase stolen cars. I tell people that when their car is stolen. I say, "Even if we do see it, and the guy takes off on us, we have to just wave goodbye."

Too bad. You are less safe with these criminals on the street. These are people engaged in lots of other felonious activity and should be put in jail. Most criminals who steal cars are out doing other things like burglaries, robberies, and drive-by shootings. Our chase policy effectively says, "If you are justified in shooting them, you can chase them." An officer has to assess whether or not a chase is justified under stress in just a few moments' time. After having months to examine it, if the city decides there shouldn't have been a chase, the cop gets screwed.

The argument for these strict chase policies sweeping the nation is that it's not worth endangering the public to catch the common criminal. I believe an argument should be made to the contrary. The buck is supposed to stop with the police. There has to be a point at which criminals are no longer able to continue on about their nefarious activities. What rarely gets out are the crimes that would have been prevented had the criminal been caught when police had the chance.

Federal and local laws were originally written in such a way where the police had the right to do what was reasonable and necessary to end conflict. Even though society has moved away from this in regard to vehicle pursuits, much of this still exists in the statutes for physical force. That's why state statutes exempt cops from charges when using reasonable and necessary force to affect an arrest. What happens is that more and more criminals are getting away and wreaking more havoc than ever before.

Rumor has it there is a small town in Texas where the sheriff has signs at the city limits that read, *If you run from the police, we will chase you.* You gotta love Texas. Maybe they're doing it right.

10
PSYCH!

Some people just believe the world is peaceful and they can't accept the reality, albeit minute, that they may fall victim to a violent crime. These people, most of my former boyfriends included, would crack under the pressure of seeing the horrible atrocities that people commit against one another on a daily basis, most of which don't make the evening news. They would spend the rest of their life rocking back and forth in a chair, covered in a blanket, dribbling porridge down their chin fed to them by a nurse.

That's okay with me, though. I like the fact that I shoulder the ugliness of the world. I see it for what it really is, and everyone else can go about their lives blissfully unaware. I sacrifice so others can live in peace—and it is *almost* worth it. It would be completely worth it if there was a little more understanding and not such a rush to judgment. It feels as if society's scolding, pointed finger is always at the tip of the police's nose. A little trust would be nice. We deserve it.

Many people don't trust the cops, especially today. They believe we are crooked sinners who abuse our authority. These are the same people who believe most cops are thieves, for example. I can't deny there are cops who have stolen, who steal, and there will be cops that do it in the future. The good thing is, they are in the smallest of minorities. You should take solace in the fact that the bad apples eventually get weeded out. I can't speak for every cop when it comes to stealing, but I can tell you my experience with it.

There's a good reason why officers who are tempted to steal choose not to—there is too much at stake. There have been times where I thought of stealing something. The first time it ever happened, I was working the desk at the station as a clerk. I was cleaning around the desk when I discovered the lost and found. I didn't even know we had one. All kinds of crap was in this drawer, but the only thing of interest was a CD wallet filled with some pretty good music discs. I took the thing out of the drawer and put it on the counter to take home with me. Later, one of my co-workers came up to the counter to visit and asked about the discs. I told him, "I found them in the lost and found. They're mine now. Finder's keepers."

"Are you willing to throw away your whole career?" he asked. "Are you willing to erase all the sacrifice and hard work you did to become a cop all for a few CDs?" I had never thought of it like that. I took the CDs and threw them back in the drawer. I was grateful to him for what he said, and it made a great deal of sense to me.

Since then, there have been other opportunities to steal something, and I always ask myself if my reputation and career is worth it. The answer is always "No." Even if I had the opportunity to steal millions of dollars, I still wouldn't do it. If I did, I would have to quit, run and hide in some foreign country to even enjoy it, and I love my family and my life too much to do that.

I'm not saying there aren't cops that steal—some cops do. If a cop does steal something and gets caught, not only is he throwing away his career, but also he will certainly be embarrassed when he is prosecuted and put on the six o'clock news.

Many people believe that if a cop screws up, they don't get in trouble. It's actually just the opposite. Elected district attorneys are often afraid of the perception of preferential treatment so most always err on the side of caution and charge the officer even if they don't have a strong case. Even more frustrating is that the cops are getting prosecuted in instances where if John Q. Taxpayer had done the exact same thing, he would never have even seen the inside of a courtroom.

In my time in Internal Affairs, I once sat through a municipal trial of one of our female officers accused of domestic violence. It was one of the most lacking cases I had ever seen. The only reason it went all the way to trial was because the accused was an officer. She did not take a plea bargain. She paid all of her attorney fees out of her own pocket. It took a jury just a few minutes to come back with a verdict of not guilty. When they called us to read the verdict, it was so soon after the deliberations started, I thought the jury was going to ask some questions or for more clarity. The whole trial was a total waste of time.

There was another officer who was off duty at a local golf course. He was with his buddies and got into an altercation with another guy and his friends. The off-duty officer and the other man ended up punching each other. In the end, there were discrepancies about who was the primary aggressor. The officer and his friends thought it was the other guy. The other guy and his friends said it was the officer.

What came of it? Most of the time, something like this would be chalked up to mutual combatants and everyone would go their own way. If charges were insisted upon by one of the parties, oftentimes both people are charged and it all gets sorted out in the courtroom. In this instance, there was no video evidence and no independent witnesses, yet the officer was criminally charged, but the other man wasn't. Clearly in my mind a double standard applied. What is even more frustrating than officers being prosecuted when they shouldn't be are the many instances of citizens who should have been prosecuted but are often not.

Sitting at my desk on a particularly slow day, I heard a call come out on the radio that said a fifteen-year-old girl had wandered into a business in the warehouse district and told the owners of the business that she had been kidnapped and raped. The dispatcher told us that the girl had blood on her clothing.

When we got there, she was hysterical. She was crying, shaking, and apologizing. Rape victims often apologize because they believe they are at fault. The girl was a little plump, with pale skin. She was wearing a pink hooded sweatshirt that had smeared blood marks on it. Her jeans looked relatively new and her backpack and school supplies were in good order. She said that she was standing outside of her high school when a black van pulled up. Out jumped two or three guys who pushed her into the van. She didn't remember anything except a rag being placed over her mouth, with a pungent odor that she said smelled like vomit. When she awoke, she was lying next to a fence and her privates hurt. She said she had never been to the area and didn't know where she was. She couldn't remember much.

As we went through the story again and again she would recall a couple of details here and there, which is typical for a victim of any crime. Eventually, we resolved that all we had in the way of suspect information was two or three Hispanic guys in a black van that had paint chips missing from the side. The van supposedly had rusty shelves lining the inside of it. That wasn't going to be easy to find.

My heart went out to her. I felt as though I would do anything to make her feel safe. I knew she would deal with this for the rest of her life. Her future husband, whomever that might be, would most likely have to deal with her understandable intimacy issues. The two of them would have to work through this together for what would prove to be a long time, if not the rest of her life. She might end up being overprotective of her children, and scared to do anything by herself.

The acts of a few people affect the lives of many for a long time to come. These rapists had essentially changed the world for the worse, and I wanted to find them and throw them in jail, hoping they might have to endure a similar incident while trying to pick up the soap in a prison shower.

I tried to comfort her, speaking softly. I let her know over and over she was safe, and that we would help her. I tried to explain what would happen next. She would be looked at by EMTs when the ambulance arrived, and we would need to try to find the place where she woke up. We would need the hospital to perform a rape kit on her and she would have to relive this story over and over, even though it was painful.

She was brave. She nodded as she looked to the floor, signaling that she realized the difficulty of the tasks ahead, but that she accepted them so that someone else didn't have to undergo the horror that she did. It was noble, and I was proud of her.

Her mother showed up at the business, and she was angry and rightfully so. But as we began to speak with the mother, it became apparent that she wasn't angry at what had happened to her daughter or at the perpetrators. She was angry *with* her daughter. She told us her daughter had mental problems and was in counseling. She said that her daughter had been skipping school and was overall a problem child.

This made me angry. Just because a child isn't an angel doesn't mean that they deserve something like this. Just because someone is doing something they shouldn't be, or is with someone they are not supposed to be with, doesn't mean they deserve to be raped.

Then, Mom told us something that was interesting and peculiar. She told us that a year ago, her little angel had alleged a similar event. The girl came home and accused the neighbor of raping her. She had taken some sort of transmission oil and rubbed it on her clothing to simulate blood. Mom then said something even more interesting: The girl had a friend who lived right across the street from where we found her, and she had been spending a good deal of time over there, much to the chagrin of her mother.

I took Mom into the makeshift interview room lent to us by the gracious business owners. Mom confronted her daughter right off, but she wouldn't break. She stood by her story and was continuing to cry and shake at the thought of her family not believing her. Using a line from *CSI: Miami*, Mom said that we would be able to conduct forensic research on the fake blood, and find that it wasn't blood at all, and that a rape kit would reveal that there had been no sex.

I left the room for a minute at the request of one of my colleagues, and he told me he was able to get the number of the girl's friend who lived right across the street. He had called over there and spoke to the friend and her mother. Both of them had seen the so-called victim about an hour and a half prior. She was fine, and had been over there visiting. The girl left saying she was going to catch a ride home at the bus stop nearby. Now realizing she wasn't abducted at her high school on the other end of town, I felt the blood rush to my face in anger.

Feeling betrayed and armed with this new information, I returned to the room, and for the first time in the day, I was mad. I told the girl about what I had just learned and threatened that she needed to come clean or we would file charges on her for false reporting. I explained the tremendous amount of resources that the city was expending and would have to continue to expend if she stayed with a bogus story. I explained how there were a lot of people who legitimately needed the police's help and that they wouldn't get it because we were having to look for rapists that didn't exist. She looked to the floor for a minute and asked her mother if she told us what really had happened if they could just go home. Although she was powerless to agree to such terms, Mom did anyway. The girl looked to the ground again and asked me if she could speak to her mom alone.

In the end, all we had done was waste hours of time. A girl who needed attention and obviously had some sort of mental illness had lied to us. Even though we knew the girl was now lying, we were still going to have to spend hours to collect statements. We would need statements from the business owners who found her, statements from the girl and her mother. We would have to drive across the street to get statements from everyone in the friend's house. Each officer would have to write long, detailed reports about their involvement. A comprehensive letter detailing the entire incident and everyone's involvement would need to be drafted and sent to the detectives.

Because the girl was a juvenile, she and a parent would be interviewed by investigators the following day. The detectives would then have to spend hours interviewing this girl on video, then type the whole case up in an investigative supplemental report. Then the detective would have to take the case to the district attorney, present it, and get it refused for charges. All of this still had to be completed even though it turned out the girl was a liar. Go figure.

The world has become a touchy-feely place. There doesn't seem to be any room for discipline. If it were up to me, the girl would have been charged with false reporting.

Detectives told us they would not pursue charges against the girl, as it's just not politically correct to prosecute a fifteen-year-old girl for lying. In what turned out to be the biggest injustice in my mind, the girl went home only to lie another day. There was zero accountability for her actions.

I found in my time on the job, and out of all the sex assaults I have ever investigated, that most of them were not actual rape. This doesn't bode well for my empathy of alleged rape victims. I can't count the number of times I've heard the cries of rape only to find out that it was a whore deal gone bad, sex for drugs where the drugs were never delivered. Some girls had sex with their boyfriends and then got caught by Mom and cried rape so they wouldn't get in trouble. Others were cheating on their husbands or boyfriends and got caught. A few just do it for plain old-fashioned revenge. Nevertheless, I go to every sex assault call with an open mind and assume they are telling the truth because the ones who were raped deserve my full effort. Over time, that becomes more difficult to do because each fake victim's story becomes more ridiculous than the last one.

One woman was living with her husband, her friend, and her friend's boyfriend in an apartment. This particular night, the four of them had another male over and all five were all watching television. Everyone except the wife and the visiting friend went to bed. The wife told me she was sitting on the couch with the friend when he made sexual advances toward her. She of course declined, and then tried to get up to go to bed. She told me she tripped over the side of the couch and fell on the floor. I find this particularly difficult to believe since it is rare I trip on something in my own home, and if I do, it has never been of such a magnitude that I fall flat on my face.

The woman told me that the man then straddled her, pulled her pants down (keep in mind she is laying on her stomach) and started to rape her. She had no reason for why she didn't yell for help with three other people in the same apartment. I'm sure someone would have come to her aid.

Then I noticed the pants she was wearing. They were very tight around the waist, and had a button that looked as if it were going to shoot across the room at any moment and injure someone. I asked if those were the pants she was wearing at the time of the assault and she told me they were. There is no way that while lying on her stomach, with those particular pants buttoned, that anyone could just grab them and pull them off her unusually large hips without a fight, or at least tearing the pants, but that was her story and she was sticking to it.

When I interviewed the other people in the home, the husband said he didn't hear anything. She was having sex with this guy while her husband was asleep in the next room. One thing of interest did happen, though. The other female roommate's boyfriend got up in the middle of the night to get some water, and when he came out of the room, saw the wife bent over the arm of the sofa taking it from the rear, and loving every minute of it. The only reason we were there is because the guy said out loud, "That's fucked up. I'm telling your husband." Nobody filed charges against this woman either for her false rape allegation.

Since we deal with liars all the time, it is only fitting to talk about them. Everyone lies. There are only a few people who will give up what they are really doing. I caught a guy in a house one night after responding to a burglary alarm, and asked him what he was doing.

"What are you, a fucking idiot? I'm a burglar," he said. It would be nice if that was the norm. Even though the burglar went to jail, I still have more respect for him than most of the people I've come across.

In my experience, some people are terrible liars. I love terrible liars. They make my job really easy.

One guy I pulled over didn't have a license and I asked him if there was anything in the car I needed to know about. He said there wasn't. I didn't suspect anything in particular, I could just tell he was lying, and badly.

"Things will go a lot smoother if you are upfront about things, because if I have to find it myself, you're going to be in bigger trouble," I told him.

He immediately blurted out, "My license is suspended. I don't have insurance. I left the plates on the car that belonged to the previous owner. I've been drinking, in fact there's rum in the Coke in this Burger King cup in my console. I have weed in my pocket and a bong under the seat."

Then there are the good liars. The first time I found crack cocaine, it was in a woman's back pocket. I was in training thankfully or I wouldn't have even known what the hell the stuff was. As soon as I pulled it out, the woman said, "These ain't my pants! Whose pants are these? They ain't mine!"

For a moment, I thought, "Man. Imagine the luck. Borrowing someone's pants and then finding out the owner had hidden crack in the back pocket." I'm glad I didn't say this because all the other cops around me weren't fooled and were laughing at the ridiculousness of this. I laugh now too, but that woman could have sold me a catsup lollipop when I was wearing white gloves.

Another time, I pulled over another amazing liar. This guy lied about his identity. I can't remember what name he used but he rattled it off his tongue along with a birth date and social security number that weren't his either. He swore up and down he was from Mississippi and that an ID had been issued with the information he was giving us. Unfortunately, he just didn't have the ID in his possession. I tried and tried on the computer to find the information he was giving me to verify it, and couldn't find anything. Every time I asked him again for the same information, he rattled it off just as sure as if I was asking him his ABCs. He had me convinced.

Most every person who lies about their personal information when asked over and over again will eventually screw up and start giving different answers. Not this guy. Another officer who was covering me on this stop suggested I take the guy downtown and have him fingerprinted.

This is a process we can use when we can't verify the identity of a person even if they are not under arrest. It's usually used on traffic stops. Most of the time people lie about their personal information because they think they have warrants. Often, cops go to all this work only to find out there are no outstanding warrants. We at least get to put them in jail for lying even though it's some puny city charge called "unlawful to give false information."

I was going to let the guy go. I figured, *To hell with it, there are bigger fish to fry tonight rather than waste two hours figuring out someone is who he says he is, especially since I believe him.* I chalked it up to a computer glitch. I wasn't willing to go through all that just to give this guy a traffic ticket and maybe a false information charge. The other cop who was with me was three years senior, and wasn't so convinced. He told me that I should take the guy and have him printed. We went back and forth. It was my traffic stop so it was my decision. I decided against it. This other cop asked if I would mind if he took the guy to ID him because he had a funny feeling.

"Knock yourself out," I said. The other cop told the suspect he didn't believe him and was going to take him downtown.

The man finally said, "Okay, I'll tell you my real name." He did, and he was wanted for armed robbery out of New Mexico. He was one tiny step away from freedom, with no idea how close he had come to walking away, and I had believed him.

Now, no matter who it is I stop, when they don't have ID, they get the third degree. After all, a person is supposed to have their license on them, and I sure don't want to let another armed robber go. Maybe it's easier to understand now why police can be suspicious of information people provide without any solid evidence.

If you've ever been doubted like this by an officer, it's possible he just didn't want a criminal to get away. Instead of complaining about it, please be patient until it can be sorted out. Inevitably, I'm betting there's some poor cop related to these complainers who has to hear what assholes cops are at each year's family Christmas gatherings.

11
THE ANSWER IS STILL NO!

The world has started down a dangerous road of placation and police departments are no exception. People don't like the word "No." They hate to be told we can't help them. They don't like to be told there is nothing we can do for them. Sometimes, however, we just can't. Instead of saying "No," we try to accommodate and make everyone feel better. We utter platitudes and sympathetic statements, when what we should be saying is "No."

You don't walk into Taco Bell and order a Big Mac. If you did, they would tell you, "Sorry. We don't do that here. You have to go to McDonalds." Under the police department model, they would be forced to say, "We don't make the Big Mac, that's McDonalds, but hold on a second and we'll send someone over there to pick one up for you."

Police departments are moving toward a customer service model, and my department was included in that trend. The problem is that it's tough to make people happy when you're taking money from them in the form of fines and/or revoking their freedom. People don't say, "That fine was the best $150 I ever spent. Man, what a good experience that was."

Cops don't say, "Ma'am, I'm revoking your freedom and going to put you in a ten-by-eight cell with a homeless man who hasn't showered since the Carter Administration, but would you mind filling out this survey to let us know how you would rate your experience today?"

Not only are these experiences mostly negative, but people are usually emotional when they call us. I have received calls because citizens were upset a random car parked in front of their house when they live in a city and their house is on a main public street. They believe the curb space belongs exclusively to them. Somehow, they managed to make it into adulthood without learning that a city street is fair game for anyone to park and there are no place-backs. When I tell them there is nothing I can do for them, they get mad at me and complain.

We've had other calls to summon us because a store won't refund money without a receipt or a friend owes someone money and isn't paying up. I am forced go to a place and explain to someone that nothing can be done about the twenty dollars their friend owes them. People flag us down and ask us if they can park in a particular place while the shadow of a big *No Parking Anytime* sign shields their face from the sun. The expectation is that they be told "Yes." God forbid they be told otherwise. If they are, and they don't like the answer, they will complain.

It's at this point in the process where someone from Internal Affairs should say, "Go away. You've wasted enough of everyone's time." That's not what happens, though. Instead, they ask questions like, "Was the officer rude?" "Did he swear at you?" "Did he give you a business card? He's required to, if you asked, you know. How dare he!"

I once got a complaint from the manager of a hotel because she didn't like my tone. She had been admonished by me because her room register, which is required to reflect an accurate description of who is in what room, had not been updated.

We had gone there to pick up a guy on a felony warrant. Because of the inaccurate registry, we were at the wrong door knocking and announcing, "Police! Open the door!" All the while, we had our back to the real felon's door. It's possible he was armed and we might as well have sent a singing telegram announcing our presence along with the message, "This is your chance to get away."

After realizing what happened and correcting the mistake, we arrested the guy without a problem, but that wasn't the point. I spoke to the manager of the hotel and let her know she could and should get a ticket for failing to keep up an accurate register. I decided on a verbal warning instead.

She filed a formal complaint with the Internal Affairs Bureau for discourtesy. Her allegation wasn't that I used foul language or was rude, but that she didn't like my tone and was mad I threatened her with a ticket.

The department ran with this. They took statements from everyone involved except the lady who complained. She could never be reached again after her initial phone call. They tried and tried to call her back, and stop by the hotel to visit her, but she was never there and wasn't returning anyone's calls.

This went on for over a month, and they still took the complaint. Even though the complaint was never sustained, it still went in my file and wasted the time of everyone involved. Someone should have told her to go pound sand, but they didn't. If it were up to me, I would have driven back to the motel and given her a ticket.

Police work, by its very nature, is negative. People don't generally come away from police service and recommend it to friends and family. With this fact alone, cops will get complaints just because people feel unsatisfied or embarrassed about what happened to them.

Complaints are a difficult thing to regulate in a police department. The line between not doing enough as far as investigating complaints and lowering morale by doing too much is paper thin. Internal Affairs fields a great deal of complaints about routine procedural items. These are called service complaints. For instance, many people will complain they didn't think they should have been handcuffed. Many people are handcuffed even if they are not under arrest. Sometimes it's to restrict the movement of someone who is agitated until the officer figures out what's going on. The good thing about handcuffs is that they come off as easily as they go on. If people are handcuffed and then let go, they think they were treated unfairly and then complain. My department did an okay job dismissing service complaints and not having them end up in personnel files.

Most all complaints could be reduced if officers remember to explain why it is they are doing what they are doing. "You aren't under arrest, but I'm here all by myself, and I'm going to put you in handcuffs for my safety until I figure out what is going on. These come off as easily as they go on," or something to that effect, usually quells people's irritation.

Police are required to provide a business card with their name and badge number in certain circumstances and when asked. People have learned this and now nearly everyone we arrest says, "I want your name and badge number." They think this is some new technique that may get them released. I hate this demand most when a moron at a bar approaches me and tells me to give a verbal essay on the equipment on my belt, and I don't oblige. They snap back, "You're an asshole, what is your name and badge number?" When this happens, I always want to demand *their* name, place of business, and supervisor's name, then go complain on them for calling *me* an asshole. It's those instances I wish people could be ejected from the bar by their face.

These innocuous complaints really put a damper on a cop's spirit. They happen often, and after a while, it becomes easier just to take the verbal abuse and be done with it. As a result, cops have lost respect in the public's eye because they will tolerate a great deal more than they should. Subsequently, when the police aren't respected, they are in more danger of getting hurt by someone. It goes the other way too. The public's safety is in jeopardy when they don't respect officers by not following orders. Respect doesn't mean liking someone, it just means respecting them.

If people were more accepting of being told no, departments wouldn't be fielding so many complaints. With all of these bogus complaints ending up in each officer's personnel file, cops become more timid to assert themselves.

Complaints that are serious in nature, like alleged law violations, excessive force, or other criminal activity, should be taken seriously. Each one of these must be investigated thoroughly. I'm not suggesting Internal

Affairs blow off an accusation a cop stole $300. However, when the person starts changing their story over and over, has a history of false allegations, or is found to be lying, that complaint shouldn't end up in a cop's personnel file. If complainants are found to be lying, they should be prosecuted for false reporting. That didn't happen very often in my department.

While working the desk, I took a complaint from a woman who said a gang of cops broke in and raped her. I sent the call to IAB and it was later proved to be false. The woman was never criminally charged.

Another problem is third-party complaints. These are made by people that were not involved or might not have even been present but later heard an account of an incident. These should only be allowed if the allegation is serious and/or criminal in nature. Third-party complaints for minor allegations such as discourtesy shouldn't be taken at all. It's a total waste of time, money, and resources.

I was working off-duty at a bar, sitting by the entrance on a stool. A man came up to me and told me that his friend was really drunk and needed to have a cab called for him. I had my personal cell phone, but wasn't going to make a call on it because minutes were expensive back then. If I called every time I was asked, I would be making calls twenty times each night.

I instructed the man to talk to the door guy, the one designated to call cabs for people. He even carried around a cordless phone for this purpose. This wasn't a huge inconvenience, as the doorman was standing five feet away from us with the phone sticking out of his rear pocket. That's the way we had always done things at this bar. The door guy knew the best numbers by heart, the dispatchers by name, and had the routine of ordering down. He happened to be in a conversation with another person, and this guy only waited to talk to him for about thirty seconds before storming off. About twenty minutes later, this same man came aggressively up to me, and got so close I thought he was going to hit me. He was screaming at me at the top of his lungs.

"You just sat there and let my friend drive away after I told you how drunk he was. Now he's probably going to kill someone, and you just sat here on your ass and wouldn't even call him a cab!" By the end of this, the man was standing between my legs with his finger in my face. It was obvious he had gone drink for drink with his friend all night long.

I pushed him gently backward so he wouldn't be so close and I stood up. How on earth was I supposed to know which person was his friend? He never introduced the drunk friend to me, never pointed him out, and never described him. Hundreds of people had come and gone from the bar since our initial conversation. Secondly, this man was holding a cell phone. I asked him whose phone that was, and he affirmed it was his.

"Why didn't you use *your* cell phone to call a cab?" I asked.

"I didn't want to use my phone, that's your job," snapped the man.

I explained how it wasn't my responsibility to give roadsides to every person leaving a bar, and then follow them until they got home to make sure they didn't drive.

Ultimately, people make their own decisions. I'm the one that catches them if they make the wrong one. My job isn't to make a decision as to what someone is supposed to do and then make sure they follow through on it. If a grown adult makes the decision to drink and drive, they take the chance of getting caught.

This man was still yelling, and spit was flying in my face as he lectured me on my job.

"I want your name and badge number. You just let him drive away!" the man slurred. This went on and on for a long while, until I had given my badge number to him and told him to go away before he ended up leaving the bar with my help. That never works. Eventually he had to be thrown out, but the bouncers had trouble keeping him out. The man tried several times to re-enter the bar. Every time he tried this, I came outside and told him, "Go home. The bar doesn't want you on their property anymore. If you come back or refuse to leave, you will go to jail for trespassing."

Believe it or not, he tried yet again. This time, he ran at a dead sprint into the bar, almost knocking the bouncer to the ground. Seeing no other option, I threw him in jail.

While we were waiting for the paddy wagon to come pick him up, I explained again about how I had no idea who his friend was, nor did I see a drunk man leave and stumble to a car. Obviously I would have intervened had that been the case.

The handcuffs had a calming effect on this guy. He was completely different than he was earlier. He understood, and looked at the ground and said things like, "I know. You're right. I really am sorry." We came to an understanding, and he knew he had brought all this on himself. He knew he deserved what happened to him.

Weeks later, I was called into Internal Affairs to make a statement. This was after a sergeant was paid to go to the bar and find the bouncers who were working that night and take statements. What a waste of time. I was called in last to write my statement, as is common procedure. The sergeant told me what the complaint was about, and I was truly surprised. I couldn't believe this guy, who ended up being very understanding had complained on me.

But as it turned out, he didn't complain on me. He told his friend, a doctor, what had happened that night, and this doctor—who wasn't even at the bar—decided to complain because he thought I should have called a cab for the drunk guy. Internal Affairs actually took a third-party complaint from this man.

Guess whose personnel file that remains in? Mine. Makes you want to run right out and get to work, doesn't it? As I thought about it, I realized the whole thing wasn't *really* about a cab for me. I would have been more than happy to have a discussion with the guy about why I don't call cabs because I have to pay for my cell phone. I'm not a courtesy telephone, I'm a policeman. It's not my job to arrange for transportation home for every person who has overindulged.

To me, this was more about respect and talking to people. It isn't okay to run up to a cop, get right in his face, and scream at him. If that's what happens, and the person is told "Back up," that should be the end of it. A light should go on, illuminating the thought, "What the hell am I doing?" Just because the cops are public servants doesn't mean we have to endure whatever John Q. Public sees fit. At a bare minimum, be respectful.

It's not that silly complaints are career ending, or that cops even get in trouble for them. It's a waste of time to have to be called in over and over again to write statements, justifying what was said. It's a pain in the ass to have them go in your personnel file forever. It could count against us when we apply for transfers, new positions, or promotions.

It wasn't we were derelict in our duties. It wasn't that we should have done something differently. Most of the time it boils down to people not taking no for an answer and then complaining because they believe they should always get their way.

My department tried to make things more fair by saying they would take into consideration the ratio of complaints versus arrests. Unfortunately, this all seemed to be just lip service. The number of complaints ended up being their only concern.

It's peace and quiet many police administrations want, not only on the part of the criminals, but also in regard to complaints. The ramifications from the ridiculous complaints and the department's handling of them is that officers are inadvertently encouraged to do less. An old timer once told me, "Do nothing, and nothing happens." When this mindset prevails, the streets are not as safe. We have to remember that, as a society, we have agreed-upon rules. Police are the enforcers of those rules and most often tasked with delivering the message we sometimes have to accept: "The answer is no."

12
EXCUSE ME SIR, WOULD YOU CARE TO STEP OUTSIDE?

This next topic is delicate. It requires some finesse and articulation. It will outrage some, and make others leery. Here goes…

Some people need their asses kicked. Many people believe force should never be used and that *everyone* can be negotiated with. They believe everyone is inherently good and can be rehabilitated. If that's you, I'm not sure you will ever accept my argument.

Those who live in the real world will agree that unfortunately sometimes violence is necessary to stop conflict. A few will argue that it should be used more often. Some might even argue it would be okay to use violence on a child rapist or murderer during a peaceful arrest for no reason other than what they've done. I mean, who wouldn't want to kick a child rapist in the nuts? As a cop, I wouldn't—couldn't—take this opportunity, because we are a civilized society.

How far should police take force? I had a DUI I was taking downtown one night. The man told me he was going to look in the phonebook, find my family, go to their house, and kill them. He then recited my last name as if to show me he was ready to go. I hoped he was bluffing, and all I did to him was charge him with threats. It was a measly little city charge that probably would be dismissed if he promised to behave. I never heard anything else about it. However, if I would have pulled over, got in the back seat with him, and made him scream out in pain, would he ever threaten another officer? Would that dissuade him from carrying out his threat?

I've been spit on many times—in the face, on my uniform, and once with a bloody loogie. Those people are charged with assault. After that happens, I have to do an exposure report, go to the clinic, and take medicine, shots, and have blood tests for months and months to assure I didn't contract anything. I wonder…if these people were kicked in the face, would they do that again?

Nobody wants to go to jail. It's not like the people that don't resist or don't run are actually looking forward to jail. Normally people that run from the cops *do* actually get hurt. This isn't because cops are beating them for no reason, it's because they are resisting arrest. Think about it: If a criminal is running, they are more likely to fight when caught so as not to go to jail. We are the ones standing between them and freedom.

Foot chases are one of the most dangerous situations for the police. Every year, several cops are killed in foot chases. People who have been hurt by the cops as a result of their resistance after a foot chase seldom repeat this situation. By the way, I'm not talking about beating kids for running from a house party where they were drinking. I'm talking about catching a guy and he swings or kicks at you just before you break his ribs with your baton.

Sure, people who fight with us get hurt and it is justified even in the department's eyes. For instance, a person spits on an officer and then gets tackled and put face down into the ground so they can't spit again. Any injury as a result of this action is appropriate.

Personally, I wish people got their licks when they had it coming. I'm talking about times when they threaten an officer's family. I'd really like to put the boots to someone who surrendered peacefully but just murdered his wife and children.

And just because this is how I wish things were doesn't mean I see it happen or am willing to do it. There are a lot of things I wish for. I wish I could drive down the shoulder of the highway in rush hour in my personal car, but I don't. I wish I could fly. I wish I was taller. I wish I could sleep with a new hot person every day and never contract a disease. I wish cops got paid more.

Despite all my wishes, I'm not willing to throw away my career and my life to beat one person who deserves it. If I did that, he would win in the end because I would be fired and go to jail. Plus, who knows if that would even stop him from doing it again.

Those of you who are old enough remember, there once was a time when people just whooped each other's asses and then it was over. Things were settled man to man. People got what they deserved and didn't complain about it. It was a simpler and more efficient time.

I used to go to this barber, an old Hispanic guy, who had the raspiest voice I ever had heard. He was short, fat, wore thick black-rimmed glasses and had silver on both his front teeth. He had smoked Camel non-filters three packs a day for years, and spent his days in a barber shop with little clientele while he watched an old TV from across the room.

He had found out I was a cop during conversation, which is abnormal for me to disclose such a thing. Usually I tell people I'm a dog catcher or trash collector so they don't start in with their "this one cop was such an asshole" stories, but I made an exception because I liked the guy. We were talking one day and he was telling me that a day long ago he was downtown. He was drunk off his ass, stumbling around, bothering people, peeing in alleys, and falling down. A cop came along and told him to go home.

"You fucking cops think you're so tough. You take that badge and that gun off and I'll whoop your ass. You ain't so tough," my barber recounted in his gruff voice. I thought his story was going to be another rendition of, "I told a cop off because I'm a badass." But instead, the story took an unlikely turn. My barber explained to me that the cop took off his badge and his gun belt and went over to the patrol car and locked them in there.

In a raspy voice that I can only hear in my head, my barber told me what happened next: "That cop took me in the alley and kicked the ever living shit out of me. Then he told me to go home." My barber didn't go to jail and didn't go to detox, but was just left there to deal with his wounds.

"You got your ass kicked and that's enough. So go home," the cop had explained to him. After all that, my barber turned me around in the chair, paused from cutting my hair, looked at me using my reflection in the mirror and said, "You know I deserved that."

You just don't hear that anymore. (You just don't see officers do that anymore, either.)

It would save all the taxpayers some money, teach people a lesson, clean up the streets, and rehabilitate them all in the swing of an fist. Instead, we put them in the hospital for make-believe injuries, jail them, or send them to a detox facility. We transport them, then waste court time on them, and when it's all over, they go right out and do the same thing again. Then we entertain their complaints and wonder why the mean cop wasn't nicer to them.

Here's the catch: Most of you would never need your ass kicked. You wouldn't run from the police. You would never spit on them or try to assault them. That's just not you. But *you* are the same people that, when someone who is deserving gets shocked with a Taser or hit with a baton, even when it is completely within guidelines, say, "That's messed up. Why do the cops have to do that?"

I call this transference. Most of you, when you hear of police using violence, picture yourselves being beat while going about your daily routine. This would never be the case. You would never have such a complete lack of respect for authority, the law, people, society, or anything else to ever be in such a situation. You would never have swung on a cop, or tried to shoot someone in the head while stealing their car, or hit an elderly woman with your getaway car after trying to kill a cop (yes, all those things did happen). It just would never be you. Let me give you another example.

One of the officers I worked with was on a call talking to some woman in the street when he looked up and saw a male fire a gun into a Cadillac Escalade full of people. The shooter looked up and saw the cop, got in his car, and started speeding off. The cop chased him for a few blocks, and luckily for us, the girlfriend was driving the getaway car and wasn't going to continue on a high-speed chase for her boyfriend.

When she stopped the car at a stop sign, he jumped out. The cops caught him and made the arrest with no force. The problem was that we couldn't find the gun. My colleague and his partner were walking back along the street where they had driven, in hopes of finding it in a lawn.

The first person who needed his ass kicked and didn't get it was the one who was arrested for the shooting. When the man jumped out of the car and swore at officers, daring them to shoot him, he was trying to pick a fight and wasn't listening to what he was being told. Nobody had to use any force because so many other cops were there within a few seconds, and the shooter finally decided his efforts were futile.

I arrived on the scene a few minutes later. After he was in the back of the patrol car, I told him to tell me where the gun was, and that if he didn't, if some kid picked it up and got hurt, he would be responsible. All this guy could say to me was "What gun? I didn't have a gun."

So, we were relegated to walking backward over the route to try to find it before someone else did. It was then that some neighbors came out of one of the houses along the street and pointed out a black car driving away. They told us the car was associated with the shooter and that the people in the black car had picked up the gun.

I ran back to my car, got in, chased the black car down, and pulled it over right as it was pulling into a driveway. The male driver popped out, I popped out, drew my gun, and pointed it at him. I was yelling, "Put your hands up! Don't move!"

He looked at me, let out a sound like air coming out from a tire and said, "Fuck you, man. You ain't gonna shoot me."

"Put your hands on your head and get on the ground," I told him again.

He looked at me again, let out another hiss, threw his hands in the air and was going on about me being a "punk-ass, bitch-ass cop who's always harassing people." His arms and verbal movements were implying, "Fuck you. Come and get me."

To complicate things, his mother came running out of the house yelling at us. His girlfriend got out of a parked car on the street like she had been waiting for this all day, and also started yelling. Now it was getting really dangerous. Nobody was listening, everyone was agitated and yelling, and somewhere there was a gun. I was stalling, waiting for other cars to come help me in between my repeated commands to get on the ground.

Finally, he folded his arms and leaned up against his car and said, "Fuck you, motherfucker." (The only thing I could think at that moment was that this guy also really needed his ass kicked.) When reinforcements showed up, he finally lay on the ground. Not only did he not get the ass whooping he had coming to him, but he went to the hospital afterward saying that when we twisted his arm behind his back to handcuff him we hurt his elbow, so he would have something to complain about later.

When he does complain later, they'll listen to him and say, "You poor soul. Tell us what wrongs have been perpetrated on you." By the way, he never got hit or struck, and I saw the x-rays—his elbow wasn't injured either, according to the doctor.

It turns out he didn't have the gun and incredibly, wasn't even involved with the whole thing, but he went to jail anyway. Why had he just not cooperated? Had he listened to us, he would have been inconvenienced for a few minutes, dusted off, and sent back inside to have sex with his girlfriend. In the old days, he would have received a bona fide ass kicking, and then probably would have listened next time. Instead, he'll do the same thing again, but probably worse because he was coddled for his complaining. Hopefully, when he does it again, an innocent person won't be hurt.

Now when I say this would never have been you, I mean it. Most of us would have done exactly what we were told, and things would have been over and done with. Most of us would have obeyed orders when a policeman had his gun pointed at the ready. Most of us would never require a beating because we have respect for people and rules. We would never fold our arms and stand there daring a cop to come get us; it just wouldn't happen.

I once responded to a call of an out of control twelve-year-old. When we arrived, there was this petite woman standing in the front yard. She couldn't have been over 5'2" and didn't weigh over a buck-o-five. This frail woman told us of how she had told her son to go clean his room when he got mad and punched her in the throat. I wondered why she hadn't got the belt out and whipped him till his little bottom was red, but then she told us that her son was a big guy and she was scared of him.

"How big could a twelve-year-old be?" I wondered. She waited outside while another officer and I went in to have a little chat with the lad. When I walked in, I was stunned. I thought that the freak show must be in town, and if this kid was twelve, then I was sixty. He was probably 5'9" or better and easily weighed over 225 pounds. Hell, even I was scared of him.

It was clearly another case of someone who needed to be taught a lesson. Instead, my partner and I each took an arm and pulled them into a twist lock because he was agitated and so he wouldn't kill us. We calmly told him that if he didn't start listening to his mother, we were going to knock the shit out of him. We twisted pretty hard to let him know we meant business. We told him that if he punched his mother again, we would come punch him. We had this little talk and all agreed that it would stay between us.

When his mother came in, he blurted out like a two-year-old, "Mommy, they hurt my arms. They hurt me and told me they were going to come back and beat me up." What he was alleging was akin to being hit with a tinker toy thrown by his baby sister, and then tattling. But I was still worried because parents today call us, and then when we try to help, they complain for being too rough with their little angel.

His mother looked at him, then at us, and then back at him and said, "Honey, they're the police. They can do whatever they want. Now go clean your room." And he did. In that case, even a little twisting of the arm was enough to get the job done…but if it were up to me, *I* would have punched *him* in the throat.

It sounds a bit like street justice, and I believe it is. I also believe there should be room for it in this world, but there just doesn't seem to be anymore. Beliefs aside, I was not going to throw away my career, everything I'd worked for, my freedom, and end up in jail over any of these situations.

My problem is there's too much Monday-morning-quarterbacking, and people expressing their opinions about situations they know absolutely nothing about. Minds are being made up without all the facts or without the necessary education about the law. Of course there are times when officers go too far in the heat of the moment and their conduct becomes criminal. Those instances are far fewer than people believe, and let me be clear that when it happens I believe they should be held accountable.

What has happened is that policies and regulations have gone too far. Almost every time an officer makes a mistake, a new rule is made. Every time a police story hits the news, another rule is made. Each new rule makes doing our job more difficult, makes another report necessary, creates another oversight board, creates more bureaucracy, wastes money and time, and sometimes even takes away tools we need.

Certain batons have been taken from police belts because one person used them wrong, and uniforms have changed because the old ones "looked too intimidating." Discretion is taken away from the police and now mandatory arrests are in place for some crimes even if the case is bogus and a waste of time. All because someone screwed up or a biased news story caused public outrage.

Street justice sure is controversial, and it doesn't sound right if you are yanked from your car and beaten for not signing the back of your registration. Sometimes, however, there is no proper way to right a wrong except for good old-fashioned street justice. You still doubt me? Let me try again.

My partner and I were driving through the projects one day in one of the rougher districts. It was one of the few days in my career I was riding with someone. We were driving along when we both looked over to see a guy taking a shit on the side of an apartment building.

We both looked back toward the road, as if the sight were perfectly natural. Then after a moment, we both exchanged incredulous looks as it registered what we had actually witnessed. He stopped the car and we both looked more closely. Not only was this guy taking a shit on the side of an apartment, but he was only about two feet away from the corner of the building. Around that corner, a family and some friends were trying to have a barbeque. They looked at us, we looked at them, and one of the guys from the patio threw up his arms like, "You've got to be kidding me."

I shared that sentiment and we walked up to old Winnie the Pooh and asked what it was he thought he was doing. He was a smelly vagrant who was really drunk. He had nothing besides the clothes on his back and a baseball cap on his head. Winnie couldn't seem to grasp why what he did isn't allowed.

In order to fully understand the gravity of this story, I must add that Winnie had diarrhea, and it really smelled. Sure, we could have given him a ticket and hauled him off to jail, but then somebody else would have had to clean it up. There is no way to enjoy barbequed hamburgers with a pile of steamy dung around the corner, nor could anyone enjoy food after having to clean that up.

I knew if I called a city agency to come clean the mess, they wouldn't get to it till after the weekend was over, and I knew I wasn't going to pick it up. So we did the only right thing in this situation: We made Winnie pick up his poo. Winnie was instructed to use his hands to pick it up, and his baseball hat as the collection receptacle. He looked at us angrily when he was finished, as he wiped the residue from his hands down the front of his shirt like an infant would clean spaghetti sauce from his fingers. He took his hat and walked off, and no, we didn't make him put his hat back on.

Two things are certain in this situation. First, the barbeque continued and was enjoyable, and second, Winnie will watch where he poos from now on. Even though he was drunk, I'm sure that wasn't fun for Winnie. We drove away to a standing ovation from the barbeque crowd.

13
PARENTHOOD

Surprisingly, it's the more subtle things in police work that bothered me. Things I never would have thought in a million years would keep me awake at night. It's not the car chases or the foot chases. It's the calls that should be routine. It's a subtlety that might come from the hurt glance of a victim's eye, but it's haunting for a long time. It might be trying to comprehend the life someone has lived, or the conditions in which they live, but it's usually a truth about the world I wish I hadn't discovered. It's a reality I wish could be changed. It would be nice to just wave a wand and make everything better, yet despite all the authority given to police officers, I felt powerless.

Parents are responsible for a lot of the misery I witnessed. Some are stupid, some are lazy, some don't care about their kids. There is nothing worse than to know some irresponsible drunken woman can and does have children. Not just one, either. The worst moms seem to have the most kids. In these families, there is no discipline, and there are no rules. In most cases like this, the mother isn't capable of properly caring for herself, let alone anyone else.

I'm not sure what causes these situations. It may be because that's the way they were brought up and don't know any better. Other times drugs or alcohol are the culprit. In any case, lack of rules, knowledge, and addictions make for a bad combination.

District four was busy one night and their calls were backing up, so they sent me to assist. I went to a family disturbance in a lower income part of the neighborhood. I arrived at a long, skinny house. The baby blue paint was peeling off the corners and the many cars blocking the driveway made it difficult to get to the door. As it turned out, this wasn't one house as it had originally appeared—it was two, although I'm fairly confident this was not the original design.

The second door was along the side of the house behind the main door and had the address written in black marker above a rusted, half hanging mailbox attached with one screw. Inside was a young mother and her daughter, who was twelve. The daughter was hysterical, crying and sobbing. I asked what was going on, to which Mom said, "Talk to her, she's the one that called" as she walked off to grab her cigarettes. She lit up, adding to the already thick cloud of smoke in the place.

After several minutes of calming down the girl, she explained to me that her older sister had beat her up. The older sister was gone now and the girl had no visible injuries. I made a mental note to myself that it was time to pin on my "Parenting Police" badge. I asked Mom what she was going to do about her rogue sixteen-year-old daughter. This would be the same girl who was now by herself out in the neighborhood in the middle of the night, the same girl whose mother could care less.

"She doesn't listen to me" was all she could explain in her raspy voice. Mom looked tired, physically exhausted, and her clothing was soiled and drooping off her body. I explained how the two sisters needed to try to get along and then lectured Mom at length as to what it means to be a mother.

"You're the mother here. She's your daughter. She lives in your house with your rules. You need to lay down the law." I looked over to see a cheap piece of meat in a frying pan on the stove. It looked like a beef roast, cut in half. The thing was charred black and cold, resembling an old boot that had been doused in gasoline and then torched until only the shape was barely recognizable. I asked what happened to dinner.

"I burned it. I was cooking when the girls started fighting and I forgot about it." She barked a cough. I looked around the house to see if conditions were so bad that the children would have to be placed in social services all the while wondering what side dishes were originally planned to go with the leather boot. In the end, there wasn't enough to take the kids out of the home.

After talking with Mom and the sobbing daughter, and doing about all I could, lecture-wise, it was time to leave. A second after I shut the door, it opened behind me. When I turned around, the little girl with bright red cheeks was looking at her feet. She asked shyly, "Can you help me with something?"

"What do you need?" I queried.

"I need to mail off a fine and I don't know how. Can you help me?" As it turns out, the girl had been ticketed for shoplifting at a local grocery store and was paying the restitution of $150. Apparently, she had earned all the money herself to make things right and she was now preparing to mail off her last of three $50 payments.

She was very proud of herself. "After this, it'll be all over and done with. I earned all the money myself. I just need to fill out the envelope and I don't know how."

I went back inside to help and looked at Mom. "Why aren't you helping her with this?" was the natural question that sprang from my mouth.

"I don't know how to do it either," Mom's response came as she lit another cigarette. She turned and vanished into the living room. A moment later I heard the television blaring, "Jerry! Jerry! Jerry!"

The girl showed me the fine schedule she had received from the city which had the directions on how to pay the restitution, along with all the other government red-tape. Somewhere on the page is where I found the address to mail the last payment. I sat down next to her at the dinner table. It was tough to find a place to write among the dirty dishes. We sat together as I showed her how and where to fill in the mailing address on an envelope, making her do it herself so she would learn. The next part of my lesson was to show her where her return address was supposed to go. She started writing out the numbers of the house in the upper left hand corner. When she was done, she looked up at me for approval.

"Do you know where to put the stamp?" I asked.

"No."

"It goes here, in the upper right corner." I pointed to the bare area of the envelope that was missing the postage. I thought it might be a good idea for her to send a copy of the court paper with the payment because it had her name and case number on it. I was worried the city would cash her check and somehow not give her credit for the payment.

"Be sure to make a copy of the statement at the grocery store when you buy the stamp and write *Paid in full* on it and put it in the envelope," I instructed. The little girl then produced a cashier's check I was sure she had to walk a mile or two in the snow to the store to obtain. I next showed her how to fill in the payee information on the check.

When I left, I heard the faint, grateful voice of an innocent girl behind me: "Thank you, sir. Be careful out there." Part of me wanted to take the girl home with me and raise her myself. Part of me wanted to smack her mom around. Part of me just wanted to cry. I didn't sleep well for a week.

As pathetic of a mother I believe that lady to be, I'm not sure it was a complete lack of morals that led to her incompetence. I would've bet she probably had less time in school time than I've spent sitting in a dentist's chair. I wondered if the world had chewed her up and spit her out and she was so tired from trying to make ends meet that all she could do was zone out in front of the television. Maybe she was just lazy and didn't care about her kids or herself. I guess without knowing her better I wouldn't be able to say.

Unfortunately, she isn't the only mom that comes to mind.

It was a nice day and unfortunately I would be spending it at one of the worst high schools in the state. This is a place where we stood in the halls and had to endure cries of "Want a doughnut?" The students at this school had a complete lack of respect not only for the police, but also for teachers, parents, and themselves. They walked through the halls and say smartass remarks while I stood there next to teachers who didn't say anything. The kids walked through the halls with soda, food, and iPods, all of which were against school policy. Students were routinely yelled at by staff members to take off their headphones or to throw away their McDonalds, but the orders were ignored by way of an eye roll.

I was standing in the lunchroom of this school when I saw a female student throw an empty box of candy across the room onto the floor. I stood there for a while trying to give her the benefit of the doubt to see if maybe she was waiting until she went back to class to pick up the trash. After about five minutes, I approached the girl and said, "You are going to pick up that box you threw, aren't you?"

"Pffff." She looked at me as she expelled a puff of air that was followed by, "I'll get it when I'm ready."

I thought of pushing the issue, but then decided it was one fight that wouldn't be worth the headache. If I had a chance of teaching this girl respect I might have tried, but I didn't want to get into a huge ordeal over a box of candy, so I just went back to my corner to stand only to watch her leave the lunchroom without picking up the box. What if I ended up getting in a fight with this girl? What if she refused? Then, if I tried to escort her to the principal's office and she shoved me, then it turned into a wrestling match and I had to handcuff her. I would go to the front office and explain that this girl was under arrest for throwing a box of Dots across the lunchroom. Nobody would care. In the end, it wasn't worth the hassle.

Being at this school was my least favorite way to spend an afternoon. There were a handful of students suspended every day, and I watched and listened as parents were informed of their children's nefarious activity…and they could care less. I don't know about you, but the times I got suspended, I was terrified to call my parents. The dean of my school would always make me call my dad myself and tell him what I had done, all while he sat there and eavesdropped, his happiness increasing with my fear. There was no worse torture than that. My parents certainly didn't idly shrug off the news of their son being suspended. They were embarrassed, humiliated, and assured everyone that I would pay for what I had done—and I did. Needless to say, my high school bore no resemblance to this school.

After lunch, there was a fight between two girls. It would come to light that both of them were mothers of babies who had come from the same father. The two women were arguing over this guy and got into a shoving match. Both the girls and I were standing outside the main entrance waiting for the mothers, who arrived simultaneously. *Finally,* I thought, *there will be some justice.* Surely the mothers were just seconds away from grabbing their daughters, bending them over a knee, and giving them the spanking of their lives. We would all feel vindicated and try to discern the apologies to the police and school staff that would certainly be ordered between smacks.

Both mothers started asking their child what had happened. The two girls explained by shouting over one another that their baby's daddy was really in love with each of them respectively, and not the other.

The mothers then began to fight with one another, yelling over the arguing daughters. It was a cacophony of screaming. But suddenly, all the distorted noises became clear as I heard one mother scream, "My daughter's pussy is tighter than yours!"

I couldn't believe my ears. I was awestruck, and my jaw dropped. Did I hear right? Did this mother just say what I thought she said? Surely I was mistaken.

"Oh no it isn't! My baby's pussy is tighter than your baby's pussy," the second mother retorted, shrieking for all the world to hear.

The arguing then resumed about which of the girls deserved this guy, who obviously was a walking hard-on with no sense of responsibility. It didn't really matter where the conversation went from there. It's hard to get past the pussy statement. That remains, to this day, one of the most horrible parenting stories I have in my arsenal. I thought of a way to try to sum it up or to end the story with some pearls of wisdom, but all I can do is shake my head and move on.

I don't know how it was when you were growing up, but my parents didn't believe me, no matter what I said. They would frequently ask teachers or deans, "What did he do this time?" One night my friend and I snuck out of the house. We were probably fourteen or fifteen. I was living with my mother at the time. There was this weird old woman who lived across the way. She was a nurse that worked the graveyard shift and lived in her basement. I know this because my mother had brought me over on one of her cordial visits to teach us how to love thy neighbor.

The upstairs was completely untouched, like a museum. In the finished basement was another kitchen so the cooking could be done downstairs. Those plastic floor runners covered the dark brown shag carpet starting at the door, and made it clear to stay on the path to the top of the basement stairs. It was just this old woman and her husband living in the place. He was equally as weird. Their upstairs bedroom was never used.

Instead, they built another one in the basement so they could live like hermits. To each their own, I suppose.

Back then, however, I thought that was good enough cause to do something mean to them. My friend and I snuck out of the house and let the air out of one of her car tires. We had learned how to take the valve out of a tire so we didn't have to sit there and hold the stem down while it emptied. We were pretty smart back then.

When we got back in my house, my mother was waiting for us. Her ice cold stare pierced through us as she stood in her robe. She asked me where I had been and what I had been doing. As any guilty child would, I told her the truth: "Nothing."

Mom picked me up by my shirt, slammed me into the wall while holding me off the ground, and yelled, "Don't lie to me. What did you just do?" I sung like a mafia rat, telling her not only about the tire, but about several other things I had done in the past. Mom then went and got an air pump. We didn't have a compressor. No sir, instead we had the fancy pump: the one that had a foot pedal. We used it occasionally to blow up a bicycle tire.

"Get out there and blow the tire up," my mom said as she thrust the air pump into my gut, knocking the wind out of me. If you've only used a foot pump to blow up a bicycle tire or a football, you aren't going to appreciate what happens next. If, however, you've ever had the misfortune to try to fill a car tire with a manual foot pump, you understand that this takes the better part of a night to put the air back. I stomped on that pedal with one foot and then the other. I did it so long and hard that even taking turns with my best friend was more exhausting than anything I had ever done.

My mom didn't believe me when I told her I hadn't been doing anything. She knew I was lying and beat it out of me, which is exactly what should have happened. If I ever have kids, I will beat the truth out of them too. Today's parents don't see this. They believe their children are angels sent from Heaven. Their children are all "gifted" and are going to be wildly successful, famous, or finally achieve world peace. They refuse to believe their children would lie no matter how ridiculous or unbelievable the tale. And to illustrate this, I naturally have a story.

While in the Hollywood division, I was dispatched to a disturbance, which turned out to be a party. It was a bunch of high school age kids who were all drinking. As we pulled up, the ones that could run did, and this included the girl who lived at the house whose mother had gone away for the weekend on a business trip.

We spent hours calling parents, taking kids home, and one even went to the hospital. I was angry that the girl responsible for hosting this whole debacle had run away. I vowed that she would be the one I was going to make sure paid for this mess. We waited and waited, but she never came back.

The next night, I decided I was going to go back to the house to give the girl a ticket. I knocked on the door, and a woman, obviously too old to have been there for the party, answered the door proclaiming, "Am I glad to see you. I was going to call you to come out here after what happened last night." I thought for sure she was going to tell me that she was sorry for her daughter's irresponsibility and that she would see to it that this never happened again. I thought she would tell me to take her daughter away, lock her up, and throw away the key. She didn't. Instead, she unleashed her fury on me. That's right, on me.

"Why the hell didn't you arrest everyone here last night? My daughter told me what happened, and about how the keys to the house were stolen from her purse while she was at school. She told me how she was sitting at home trying to study for her test when the thieves came and broke in, and then invited people over to party at the house. My daughter told me that she begged and pleaded for them to leave and how more people just kept coming. I want them all arrested for trespassing and burglary!"

I stood there astonished, and I mean truly astonished. I was having trouble composing a response to this tirade. Could this woman possibly believe her daughter's story? So that's exactly what I asked her, but my question just bounced off of the woman.

"You didn't do anything. You just let them all go. My daughter is lucky she wasn't killed or raped. I want them all arrested!" The fire in her breath was now roaring. I told this woman as firmly as I could, "You can't possibly believe that your daughter didn't throw that party. Did she tell you about how she ran away and hopped the fence, abandoning her friends and her home when we came? Did she tell you about how there were flyers passed out at the school the day of the party inviting everyone?" I happened to have one of the flyers with me and I shoved it into the woman's hands.

"Well...she...she couldn't have arranged this thing. My baby wouldn't do that," the woman insisted, staring down at the paper.

"Sure she wouldn't," I mumbled as I handed the mom a citation with all the charges on it. "Take your little angel to court." I turned and walked away.

14
JUST THE FACTS, MA'AM

Joe Friday used to say, "Just the facts, ma'am." It would be nice if we had all the facts before we arrive somewhere. As officers, we often have to react based on very little information. To compound the situation, the people we are dealing with are usually angry and can be volatile and dangerous. And the trifecta for officers is that most of the time things evolve very quickly. This combination makes situations more dangerous and certainly scarier to walk into. Instinct and training take over and we are forced to just react. I have had times where my gun has just appeared in my hands and I wondered, "How did this get here?"

This happened to me for the first time on a domestic violence call. The front door buzzer system was broken, but luckily for the victim in this case, so was the lock on the entry door. As I entered, a male teenager came running up behind me from the outside of the building, and as I turned around I noticed he was out of breath and sweating. He looked up and politely said, "Excuse me" as he continued into the apartment building. Now I wasn't a detective at the time, but nonetheless, it struck me as a possibility that this person could have something to do with this domestic to which I had been dispatched. I told him to stop and asked what apartment he was going to.

"204" was his reply. Coincidentally, it just so happened that was the same apartment I was supposed to go to.

"What's going on?" I inquired.

"My sister's getting her ass kicked and I'm going to help her," exclaimed the boy, nearing a panic.

"No you're not! I am." It was all I could manage to come up with at the time. I felt an urge to adjust my cape and puff out my chest, revealing the red and yellow "S" that was there.

I patted him down for weapons because for all I knew, he had brought a gun with him to kill the guy who was beating his sister. This thoroughly pissed him off.

"What the fuck are you doing, asshole? My sister's getting her ass kicked."

To me it didn't seem all that unreasonable that this brother was coming over to seriously hurt the sister's lover. It also seemed plausible that he had armed himself with some sort of weapon just to make sure he didn't lose. To me, my request was mundane and perfectly logical, but I understood how he felt. He wanted me to go help his sister, not treat him like a suspect.

I know what you're thinking: "You didn't have to frisk him, just tell him to stay there and go upstairs." Some of the *really* naïve might have suggested taking the brother with me to assist.

"Come quick, Robin, we'll save her!" I would say to my new sidekick. The two of us would go upstairs and I would grab the lover, then the poor, beaten sister would say, "Leave him alone!" while she started to hit me. I would then shove her away so she couldn't hit me, and that would anger the brother, at which point he would yell, "Don't hurt my sister!" and produce a tire iron from his pants and knock me unconscious.

What if I got up there and grabbed the poor, beaten sister and then the brother was so intent on getting even he pulled a gun and shot the abusive boyfriend? I was also worried that I would tell the brother to stay downstairs, but later find he would surreptitiously follow me up there, whip out a knife, and start shanking someone. It's not too far-fetched that he could have accidentally hurt himself, me, or his sister with the weapon he might have brought. It's also possible he might get his weapon taken away by the abuser who then used it against all of us. To avoid all of these scenarios, I thought it wise to make sure he didn't have any of the aforementioned items.

These pat-down or cursory searches are conducted for the sole purpose of officer safety. Contrary to popular belief, they don't require a warrant. They are necessary and important. On any call, I don't want to stand around and talk to a group of people while they put their hands in and out of different pockets without first knowing they aren't grabbing for a weapon. After all, I have never met any of these people before, know nothing about them or their past, and have no idea what any of them are capable of doing to me or others.

After my brief search of the brother turned up nothing, he said, "Well get the fuck up there! Can't you hear her screaming?" I could indeed hear screams, and I instructed him to stay in the entrance and told him if he came upstairs, he would go to jail. After all, it's common in these domestic situations, as I mentioned, to have the victim turn on you when you attempt to stop or apprehend the abuser. The last thing I needed was the girl's brother up there to complicate the situation. To this day I'm amazed he obeyed. In a perfect world, I would have cuffed him to the door to assure he stayed downstairs, but that would have landed me in hot water. At least having searched him, I now knew even if he did come up, at least he didn't have a weapon.

I went upstairs, and as I got to the second floor, I could still hear a woman screaming. I went to the door and could hear what sounded like a major battle going on inside. Screaming, yelling, and thumping echoed from inside the apartment. My heart started to beat because this was obviously no routine domestic. I got on the radio and told the car that was sent to cover me that he needed to step up his response to code 10. It is uncommon and not recommended to enter a domestic violence alone, although it is routine whoever gets there first to listen at the door to determine the validity of the call. In a situation where the woman might die or be seriously injured if a cop waits for cover to arrive, I know most of us would enter alone no matter what the risk. I didn't even have time to have to make that decision.

Just after I told my cover car to come code 10, the door flew open and a woman ran out into the hall screaming. I looked in the apartment and saw the woman's boyfriend charging with a ten-inch serrated kitchen knife, the kind with the two tiny prongs on the end. I was speechless. I don't recall drawing my gun, but I found myself suddenly holding it in my hand.

One thing was certain: All the "Police, freeze!" or "Stop or I'll shoot!" lines I had practiced all those years were nowhere to be found. My mouth was open and the only sound I could make was one similar to a horse trying to blow the snot out of his nose.

He was about ten feet away from me and still running full speed ahead. The rule we were taught in the police academy with regard to knives is known as the twenty-one foot rule. This has been scientifically proven. Basically, a person within twenty-one feet of you who has a knife can get to you and stab you before you can draw your gun, fire, and (the most important part) stop him. This man was clearly within the twenty-one feet and judging by his speed would soon be able to gut me like a fish. I was raising my gun at the man when he saw me, fell to his knees before me, threw the knife, and put his hands in the air. We stood there for a minute, the tip of my gun quivering at his body, him wide eyed and staring at me. I kept him at gunpoint until my cover arrived and we cuffed him and took him to jail.

One of the problems with this job is that I rarely find out what happens on most cases. The detectives are the ones who follow up on the investigation and actually meet with the district attorney to file the charges. Sometimes I have to testify at trial, but most of the time I put myself on-call and never get called because of a plea bargain. Sure, I could have followed up on the outcomes of these stories, but I typically never did.

This domestic was one of the rare cases I had to testify. In this case, he was found guilty. I remember talking to the victim outside the courtroom after the trial. To this day she is the only woman victim of a domestic I know of who actually left a man for good after being abused. I believe her exact words were "That motherfucker is gone with a capital 'G.' I ain't talked to him since. He keeps trying to apologize and shit, but ain't no motherfucker gonna do that shit to me and come back in my house." That still makes me smile.

There have been a few instances where I was waiting for a long time to see what was going to happen. These situations are the scariest because they evolve to the tensest of moments and then just hover there for what seems like eternity. There is all kinds of time to think not only about what has to be done, but also about all of the different possible outcomes. If there's ever a time I wished I was on a tropical island with sandy beaches and some sort of drink served in a piece of fruit, this would be it. I always think, *If I get out of this, I've got to take a vacation.*

I was hauling ass to cover officers one summer afternoon on a barricaded suspect who was armed. I was there shortly after the call came out as the first officers realized the magnitude of the situation. When I arrived, I took a position of cover behind a cement pillar. Tons of officers had already arrived and the place was surrounded.

When we had a barricaded suspect who is armed, the SWAT team had to be called out. While waiting for them to arrive, this crazy asshole inside the basement apartment was yelling at us. I was about five feet away from a cement stairwell that formed a path to the basement apartment where this guy was located. It was the only door to get in the place.

I took a position behind the cement pillar holding my gun at the ready for what seemed like an eternity. Lots of psychological and physiological things happen to an officer's body in a time like this. Remember when you used to play hide-and-go-seek as a kid? The only time you had to pee was right at the moment you got settled in your hiding spot. That happened. Your body fatigues.

You try to hold a .45-caliber loaded gun in front of you for ten minutes and see if your hand doesn't tremble. Your mind starts thinking about all the outcomes. It's one thing to have to shoot someone; it's another to be told that in a few minutes you're going to have to shoot someone. It's an awful thing to sit with.

"I ain't goin' to jail. You motherfuckers are gonna have to shoot me. You better get ready, I'm comin' out shootin'." The whole time, other officers were trying to talk him out peacefully. Nobody had any idea why he was so distraught and he certainly wasn't telling us.

"You ready, fuckers? Here I come! Get ready. I'm coming out shooting." This went on and on, and I was becoming less and less confident in my now fatigued, trembling hand.

The door swung open and a man came running up the stairwell screaming like a kamikaze pilot. There must have been seven cops within a few feet of me. We were all shocked and trying to figure out what he was going to do. It was all happening so quickly.

Where's the gun? Does he have a gun? Where's the gun? Is there anything shiny? Is it in his pants? Where is it? Hurry up and find it!

I waited to hear gunshots. He got all the way up the stairs and basically ran into us. As we collided, we wrestled with him until we could get him handcuffed. Nobody shot and he didn't even have a gun. I'm still amazed because if a cricket had farted, we all would have started shooting and not stopped until he had stopped charging us. He was attempting suicide by cop but thankfully this time nobody was hurt.

More common are the many people who commit suicide without involving the police. Some are in a desperate depression, are miserable, and in constant pain and agony. Many of these people don't know how to get help or reach out to the resources available to them. We try our best to get these people help before it's too late. This is why we take so seriously outcries from anyone about people who are talking about suicide.

Another type of suicide is someone who is trying to teach someone else a lesson or make others feel guilty. I was on one of these scenes once. It was obvious because of the suicide note. The guy was heartbroken about their breakup. The tone of the note was such that it was intended to make the woman think this was all her fault.

The guy was lying in a chair with his head slumped over to the side—he had been playing a game of Russian Roulette. In his lap was the gun. There was a slow drip of blood to the floor. The old timer cop with me said, "Boy, you sure showed her."

The hardest suicides to process for me are the senseless ones like where somebody thought their predicament was worse than it actually was. A college boy was home for summer break. Before the semester ended, there had been a wild night of partying. The melee resulted in a mini riot where police were forced to disperse tear gas. Some of the agitators were made an example of and charged with inciting a riot, which is a felony.

He was facing the charges when he returned to school, and had yet to appear in court. Instead of seeing what the outcome was going to be, he decided to go out in the backyard and blow his head off with a shotgun. His mother found him. What a terrible thing to do to your parents. According to his suicide note, this kid killed himself because he believed his future was ruined since he had been charged with a felony. He thought he was going to have to go to jail and never be able to get a good job. Most likely he would have got a deferred sentence or a plea bargain, done some community service, and moved on. How sad.

As far as officer safety goes, a suicide is usually over by the time we get there. Suicides aren't usually rapidly evolving situations. There is an exception to this, and that is an active suicide *attempt*. These situations can and do change quickly. The difference between life and death could be only a matter of seconds.

Some suicide attempts get called in as something different and the officers are blindsided when we arrive. Three of us were walking up to a house one night on what we were told was a domestic. The call sounded like a bogus one with very little information. I rang the doorbell and the other two officers were behind me chatting about who had better hash browns, Village Inn or Denny's. I was trying to look through a distorted glass pane on the side of the door to see when and if someone was coming to answer the door.

I could see inside fairly well. Ahead of me was an empty living room. The place was very nice and clean. It looked like a normal house. I was waiting and waiting, nobody was coming to the door, so I rang the doorbell again.

From the hallway out walked a man in his underwear. He was holding a long knife with blood all over it and his arms. He was walking like Frankenstein on sedatives, hunched over with a glazed stare.

He made it just out of the hallway and barely into the living room when he stopped. To his right was the opening to the kitchen. He paused for a moment, slowly looked toward the front door and then back toward the kitchen as if deciding what he was going to do.

There was no doubt in my mind that this man had just cut up his wife in the bathtub. I pulled my gun, I think I yelled, "Holy shit," and I kicked the front door in. Normally, I would have stood there for a moment being impressed that it only took me one kick, but there was no time.

The two cops behind me snapped to attention and followed me in, knowing something must be very wrong. We got to the man quickly and were able to put him in cuffs without any problem. A moment later, from out of nowhere, came a woman who was scared and upset, but not cut up into pieces. She told us that her husband was distraught about the two of them separating, and that he had went into the bathtub and tried to slit his arms. Judging by the gouges all the way up both forearms, he had done a pretty good job. He had cut both arms from the wrist up to the elbow joint. We had to go with him to the hospital and learned he wasn't going to die.

That night, I learned that things are not always as they appear. It's human nature to make snap decisions based on the little we see or hear. It's just the way we are all designed. Please keep this in mind when you judge the actions of police later with the benefit of hindsight. Also know, you probably don't have all the facts about what occurred and what was known at the moment the police acted.

15
THE EMERGENCY ROOM

I was brand-spanking-new. Wet behind the ears, green as lettuce, and a brand new boot. I was sitting in the parking lot of a golf course driving range at the farthest reaches of the city. A call came out about a naked man running through one of the more suburban parts of town. I know what you're thinking—and no, I didn't go just to see a naked guy. So I started heading to the call. I was thinking as I sipped my Starbucks that it was probably some stupid idiot who lost a bet, or was dared to streak across the neighborhood naked. While I was on my way, the dispatcher told me that she was getting several calls on this. Then she updated me that he went into a woman's house and was running around. A few moments later another update came that he had torn the screen door off of another woman's house. I was beginning to think this was no college prank.

I was the first officer there. Of course, I had no trouble spotting a 6'6" naked man running around. This man was huge, resembling Andre the Giant. He had the same black greasy, curly hair and looked similar in stature. The similarities stopped, however, when I looked closer. This man had pierced his penis with a silver rod, and it was definitely not a professional job. This begs the question, "What kind of person would sit around bored at home and decide to pierce their penis with a silver metal rod?" I still don't have the answer to that.

Then I looked at his chest, where he had cuts that were about the same length and angle as the scars on Rambo's chest, except there were many more of them, and they appeared to barely be scabbed over. Obviously they weren't too old. This man looked at me and I looked at him as I ran behind my patrol car. He raised his arms in the air and roared like a beast.

I thought, *Fuck this*. So I took out my gun and ordered him to get on the ground. I was hoping the intimidation of me going straight to my gun would scare him enough to listen to me. That never works. He just roared again and then ran away from me, which I was glad at least he didn't charge right at me.

There was a fountain in the middle of this neighborhood as part of the landscaping, one with water shooting up from the center of a small pond. The pond was circular, a little bigger than a kid's blow-up swimming pool, and only about mid-shin deep. He stood in the pond and stopped to face me. I was about fifteen yards away.

Looking back, I should have just waited for other cops to arrive. I got on the radio, and for the first time ever, I said, "Send me everyone you have code 10." The dispatcher sounded the alert tone, or "toned it out" as we would say, and did a simulcast to the whole city.

My city prides itself because emergency cover to officers usually occurs within a minute. Not on this day. I was in the southern part of the city right at shift change. They broke the roll call of the afternoon shift to come help and sent neighboring districts, but it would still prove to be almost ten minutes before anybody got there. Ten minutes is a long time when you're fighting. That's over three Red Mans in a row!

I looked up at the naked man. I knew I couldn't shoot him, although at the time I wished I could have. I started to approach, and he picked up a decorative river rock and put it in his mouth. A moment later, he roared once again, and I couldn't help but notice that the rock was no longer in his mouth.

"Did this crazy fuck just eat a rock?" I think I actually said that out loud. I approached him and unleashed my entire can of pepper spray on him, a tactic that would soon prove to be one of my least favorites. I had to learn the hard way that when spraying the stuff, it's better to be upwind so it doesn't blow back in your face.

As I was choking and gagging, old Andre didn't seem to have been affected much. The only result the pepper spray had was to make this man roar again and then start to run off.

The first cover officer arrived. We again called for cars code 10.

By this time, we had amassed quite a crowd of spectators from the complex. Andre was running right at the crowd, growling and roaring. It appeared as if he was going to hurt or maybe even kill one of them. I took out my full-length wooden baton, and just as I was taught, tried to hit him in the approved places. We are taught not to hit people in the knees, head, groin, kidneys, or other sensitive places. I hit him in the legs below the knees and above the knees in the thigh. As he was walking away from me, I would take a couple of steps' running head start to catch up to him and gave it all I had. He didn't fall, and he didn't stop. He was getting closer and closer to this crowd of people, and I truly thought that he was going to kill one or more of them. The other cop who was with me said, "Fuck that academy shit, he's going to kill someone. Hit him in the knees." I hit him twice as hard as I could. He didn't fall and he didn't stop.

The other cop intercepted Andre before he got to the crowd and began to wrestle him to the ground, and I quickly tried to help. This would prove to be the second downfall of pepper spray—when someone is sprayed and then wrestled with, it gets all over everyone and starts to burn everywhere.

We wrestled and grappled and were able to get one handcuff on him. I felt victorious when we did this and was ready to leave calling it a job well done. It was at this point the question ran through my head as to why none of the people we just saved were coming to help. Finally, one man out of the group of spectators ran over to assist. With all due respect to him, and as much as I appreciate that he came over to help us, this man was older than Moses. The three of us were trying to latch on the second handcuff when Andre stood up and threw all three of us off of him. He was now swinging around his arm with the one cuff on it, and the other metal end was flying around and nearly took us out.

I decided enough was enough, and I thought our only chance to stop him was to choke him. That's not the proper way to refer to this technique. The method is actually called the Carotid Compression Technique. This is where a person's blood supply to the brain is cut off. It supposedly takes about ten seconds to render someone unconscious. The thought here is to not choke them or crush their windpipe (as this might kill them), but the inside of the elbow goes over the Adam's apple to protect the larynx. That way they aren't actually choked, but they go unconscious. The problem was that he was too tall to get my arm around his neck.

So I jumped on his back, wrapped my legs around his waist, and started trying to apply this technique. I tucked my head into his so he couldn't lurch back and head-butt me. Based on the choking noises, I was pretty sure I wasn't doing it right, but I knew that if I let go I would fall or be hurt, so I held on as long as I could.

It took a lot longer than ten seconds for anything to happen. At this point it was reaffirmed that I had no desire to be in a rodeo. Andre was trying to violently buck me off and spin around to get me off of him. I just held on.

After what seemed like an eternity, old Andre fell to the ground and began losing strength. The other cop and the old man secured the second handcuff just as the other officers began to arrive.

I was exhausted, I really was. An ambulance came and they put him in the back. A few minutes later he must have regained his strength. Good thing they had him tied down to the gurney. I looked over to hear the roars of an awakened beast as the ambulance rocked back and forth like the Tasmanian devil was inside. At that time, the paramedics were able to use what's called a chemical restraint. Nighty-nite Andre.

I later found out Andre had overdosed on several different drugs, had a brain hemorrhage, and almost died (I didn't hear that from a doctor, so take it with a grain of salt). The near-death experience wasn't a result of the fight with the police, but was because of the level and types of drugs in his system.

I went to the hospital after this ordeal because when we went to the ground, something hit me in the balls. I'm still not sure what it was. I got scared into going to get checked out. I didn't want to go but the other officers told me if I didn't get checked and it turned out later I had an injury, the city might not cover it. Nevertheless, I've never had that many people look at my testicles in one day.

I remember the head doctor coming in. "Let me have a look." He wanted to make sure I got the royal treatment. Part of me was beginning to wonder if my balls were abnormal and every person that checked them went out and told the other doctors, "You gotta see this kid's balls." This was the first time I had been to the hospital on this job, but it wouldn't be the last—luckily nothing too serious.

I went one time for a car accident, and no it wasn't my fault. Another time I was exposed to whooping cough, and had to take an antibiotic that made me throw up all night. I think I would have rather had the cough. I have never wished so hard for two toilets adjacent to each other, one for each end, but instead I was relegated to quickly switching as needed, tying to flush in between so as to not make things worse.

When I think about being injured on the job, I realize there are millions of ways that could happen. Literally. One officer I know went to the hospital after being bit by a spider while trying to crawl through a window. Cops even accidentally hurt each other. This next case of "friendly fire" just goes to show how vulnerable we are at any time, even when we think it's safe.

A whole slew of cops had a house surrounded where a bad guy was barricaded. The call started with two guys who had run from a stolen car. One had been caught outside, and the other was inside. We were holding the perimeter of the house so we could send in the dogs. This is always my preferred method of catching people inside a house because I don't want to go in and have to check every little nook and cranny. In that kind of situation, the bad guy always has the advantage. (Looking under beds is my least favorite. If the mattress and box-spring can't be thrown off the frame, there's no other way to check underneath besides to drop to the knees and look under the bed. If someone were under there with a gun, I would have a third eye before I even knew what hit me.)

I never would want to see a police dog shot, but it's better than one of us. When the two dogs got there, a few of us went in with the dog handlers. One dog went upstairs with a couple of cops. The second dog, the handler, another cop, and I went downstairs. Most of the basement was clear, but then there was a little workshop area of the basement that hadn't been finished. There was a makeshift table made from two-by-fours and an old countertop. On top were stacks and stacks of boxes. Underneath were even more. Nothing looked disturbed to me. Under the table, behind all the boxes, was the entrance to the crawl space. The dog was going berserk trying to get at the crawl space. It didn't look like anyone could have gotten in there and then rearranged the boxes in front of the hole while inside the crawl space. The dog handler was positive that his dog knew better.

The dog handler was giving the standard warnings before releasing the dog. Nobody answered and nothing could be heard. During all of this, the other dog and his handler had finished their search upstairs and had come down to see if they could help us. I was standing in the entrance to the unfinished work area waiting for the dog to do his thing.

Before I knew it, it was like the gates had opened at a greyhound track. The dog was running full speed, knocking boxes out of the way as he forged his way into the crawlspace without the slightest bit of fear. The next thing I heard was a growl, and then the suspect's scream. At that exact moment, I felt something hot tingle in the back of my own right arm, followed by a stinging sensation. As I looked around to see what had happened, I noticed the other dog was now swinging from my arm. I've always heard stories about how when people are shot or stabbed, they often don't know it because the body releases chemicals to protect itself against pain. Obviously that part of my brain was on a smoke break because that bite hurt like hell.

The dog handler wrestled his dog off of me as the other dog was being wrestled off the guy from the crawl space. The crook got it worse than I did because the dog who bit the suspect actually dragged the full-grown man out of the crawl space by his leg. It was amazing to watch. It would have been more amazing if I didn't have to fight off my own dog attack.

It was later that day, after I processed the whole incident, I decided that if ever on the run from the cops and I heard a dog, I would give up. Luckily the wounds in my arm didn't puncture anything that wouldn't heal after a short time. It was also lucky that my arm looked much better than the suspect's leg.

Coincidentally, this was also the same day I decided I don't like emergency rooms. I didn't appreciate the nurse sticking those cotton swabs with the long wooden sticks down into the holes in my arm. I really didn't appreciate her twisting it back and forth quickly while simultaneously pulling up and down, like she was cleaning the barrel of a gun. As soon as she started, I inquired as to why anesthesia hadn't been used. I asked that in a joking manner because other cops were in the room. While they laughed along with the nurse, I couldn't help but think to myself, *I was serious.*

To make the whole matter worse, over the next week, the dog handler responsible for my bite told a different story about what had happened. I would soon learn K-9 officers don't want their dogs biting other cops because, if it happens repeatedly, they may lose their dog. At the bare minimum, nobody will want to go with them on calls if it gets around that Scruffy will bite any officer in the vicinity. It was because of this that the dog handler told my co-workers it was my fault for jumping in front of the dog while the other dog was biting the suspect.

I can tell you with one hundred percent certainty that all I was doing was standing in a basement doorway when my arm became a dog biscuit. I didn't even know the other dog was that close to me. The whole thing added insult to injury, literally, as now I had to go around trying to tell everyone I hadn't jumped in front of his dog so they wouldn't think I was an idiot.

One of the other K-9 handlers caught up to me a week later and explained the whole thing about how the handlers don't want to admit if their dogs screw up. He took some extra time to explain a little more about the K-9 psyche. Hearing the first dog bite the suspect really excited the second dog, who wanted in on the action and latched on to the closest thing to him—my arm. I didn't take much consolation in this explanation, but it was better than nothing.

I love dogs, I really do, but after this little incident, I was never the same. Even to this day, I find myself being scared of many dogs. A week after the incident, I was at a water fountain in a park when a little dog no bigger than Toto came up to my feet and began barking. I must have jumped ten feet in the air and screamed like a girl. Talk about feeling foolish. I mumbled something to Toto's owner about a K-9 dog and my elbow, which I'm sure made no sense. I walked off hoping if I kept my head down, the woman would never recognize me, and never be able to point me out to her friends—"There's the stupid guy who was scared of my five-pound dog." That's when they all would point at me and laugh.

I definitely didn't expect to get hurt on that last call because I thought the dog was going to do all the dirty work, but there are some calls like this next one that I'm surprised nobody was hurt at all. A burglary-in-progress came out late one night. The wife was upstairs on the phone with 9-1-1 saying that she could hear her husband in the basement fighting with an intruder that had broken in while they were sleeping.

I pictured my own mom scared to death and my dad downstairs fighting for their lives. Two other cops and I arrived at the same time and went into the house. The wife let us in and was horribly upset because it was quiet down in the basement. I'm sure she was wondering along with all of us whether or not her husband was already dead, and the bad guy gone.

As we walked down the stairs, the first thing I noticed was a white guy with a mustache. He looked exactly as if he had escaped from the penitentiary about twenty minutes prior. It was the kind of guy that looked like he spent all of his time in the yard lifting weights. He was stocky, had tattoos on his arms, and looked like he could beat almost anyone in a fight. He was wearing clothes that were about thirty years out of fashion.

As I took in more of the scene, this same jailbird (who I later found out didn't escape, but had been out of prison about as long as it takes to make toast) had something shoved in his mouth. It was black, shiny, and long. As I followed the tube out of the guy's mouth, I saw it was attached to a cylinder with bullets in it, and then the dark handle of a gun appeared.

I then saw the hammer was cocked back. Holding the gun was Ward Cleaver himself. No disrespect, but the homeowner wasn't exactly runner up in the World's Strongest Man Competition. He was just an average, short, upper-middle-aged guy with a comb-over who probably drank a few too many beers in his day. The homeowner was gripping the revolver with one hand and with the other had the intruder pinned up against the wall by his throat. The intruder was a two-pound trigger pull away from being a brain collage. Instead of screaming, "Help me! Help me!" the homeowner simply looked up and said, "Come and get him fellas, he's all yours."

The basement had a broken coffee table and obviously looked as if the two had thrown each other around a bit. The astonishing thing about all this was that the homeowner didn't just go downstairs, confront the burglar with a gun, and then stick it in his mouth. Instead, the two fought and tussled for a bit before Mr. Cleaver won out. Nobody was hurt and nobody went to the hospital. It was the opposite of how I thought things would turn out.

Bottom line is I've been lucky. So many cops have been and continue to be hurt far worse than I ever was. Officers can never predict when or what calls are the ones that will land them in the hospital. Other times officers responding to similar calls are reminded of their past injuries. They don't want it to happen twice, so they do their best to protect themselves and others from injury. Knowing why officers might be defensive when they deal with you is because we just never know. That's why it's so imperative to always be on guard—this mentality saves lives.

16
I'LL TAKE STUPID COPS FOR $1,000, ALEX

You must be thinking by now of your own police stories in which all of my explanations can't render a dumb cop smart. Now there aren't many of them thankfully, but there certainly are a handful of idiots on the job. What would this book be if I made fun of everyone but us? After all, we have to be able to make fun of ourselves, remember? Just for good measure, I'll include the dumbest thing I ever did too, but I'll save that for last.

Sure, we've all done something stupid. Most of the time cops do stupid stuff, they're overzealous. Each of us tries so hard to enforce every law and make such a difference that sometimes we end up making asses of ourselves.

I was standing on a famous street notorious for hookers, talking to a known one. It is common to stop and either try to talk prostitutes out of their lifestyle choice or to try to get the 4-1-1 on what new criminal activity might be in the area.

A boot cop pulled up and was watching me in action. As we were talking, a bicyclist rode by on the sidewalk, and right in mid-conversation, this newbie diverted his attention and yelled at the bicyclist, "Hey! You can't ride your bike on the sidewalk. Get back here!" Then, he actually started to run after him. I yelled the cop's name and had the little talk about why it was we were going to leave the bicyclist alone. I mean here I was about to find out about all the major crime and criminals in the area and this guy is getting in a foot pursuit over somebody riding their bike on the sidewalk. (Don't tell my superiors, but that's one I don't enforce because riding a bike in traffic is terrifying. It feels much safer on the sidewalk even though technically it's illegal. Despite the law, if you ever spot me on a bike, it will be on the sidewalk.)

Another poor officer (who probably still takes a ribbing about this) was with a DUI suspect on the side of the road as another cop drove by (that's how we got the story). The cop passing this situation at highway speeds only could tell us that the man in custody for DUI was peeing on the shoulder while in handcuffs.

As you may or may not know, suspects are almost always cuffed with their arms behind them. The question then struck the passing cop: "How could a guy in handcuffs get his pants undone, take his penis out, pee, and then pull them back up without any help?" Later, the officer tracked down the cop responsible for the arrest and asked how the prisoner had managed this.

Now, there are two things you need to know. First, I have had several DUIs pee in the back of my car. One of them urinated on my coat another cop had ignorantly left in the back seat. Not only did he put my coat back there, but he also sat our prisoner on top of it. It's a real pain in the rear to have to call out the decontamination people, especially on a graveyard shift.

Needless to say, I understand wanting to accommodate someone who says they are going to pee in the back seat if they don't get to a bathroom. Secondly, when telling a lie to co-workers, especially cops, it better be a good one. I found out fast on this job that one of the best ways to stop any rumors about you is to strike first.

I was new in the district, and the cop who already had been dubbed "The Penis Holder" found me at the 7-11 to try to strike first with his version before I heard the other side, but he was too late. He explained to me that nobody understands what had happened, and that I might hear things about him that aren't true. He told me that he had a DUI one night and that the prisoner said he was going to piss in his back seat if he didn't get to a bathroom. All okay so far, but then this was his explanation for what happened next: "I got the guy out of the car, and he wiggled his pants down, peed, and wiggled them back up."

I've seen enough episodes of *Mr. Wizard* in my day to know that defies the laws of physics, logic, and gravity. I'm not sure and never will be about what really happened there on the side of the road. Maybe the guy was able to urinate without help from the officer or being taken out of handcuffs. I do know it would be a safety breach of the highest degree to uncuff a prisoner by yourself on the side of a roadway. Even if the officer did help him, I'm sure he was totally disgusted by it and even haunted by the memory of the whole incident.

If that ever happened to me, I would make sure backup was there, then take the guy out of his handcuffs to handle his own weenie. If nobody could come help, I would just get the car cleaned afterward. Hopefully this time my coat would be in the front.

There are a few other cops, however, who aren't overzealous, but who just do dumb things. They are the nicest people and have the biggest hearts, but man-oh-man I do not like to be around them at work. Fortunately for all of us, these next few stories are all from one person in particular. The guy would give you the shirt off his back, but hopefully isn't involved in your police activity.

This cop was screaming into the radio one night on the scene of an accident for more cars to help him. It wasn't uncommon for him to scream into the radio when anything happened, but this one sounded especially serious. We were coming in expecting to see the worst of accidents. He was directing us all in and having the roads closed and traffic diverted. When I got there, all the other police had the road closures handled, so I went to assist the screamer. He was standing at an accident in front of a house with about twenty people around him.

A car had run off the two-lane road and hit a parked car along the curb, the same car that belonged to someone in the house. They were not happy to say the least. The right lane was partially blocked with the rear of a car, and the left one was completely unobstructed. Nobody was hurt.

Why was the road closed and traffic being diverted? This was essentially a two-car, no-injury accident with moderate damage. Why was this man screaming into the radio like he was being shot from a cannon? When I pulled up, I thought for sure maybe the crowd of people from the house may have become agitated or aggressive.

As it turned out, they were mere spectators and had made peace with the fact one of their parked cars was wrecked. I got out of my car still baffled at what was causing his panic. He looked at me, stopped his interview with the driver, and began yelling at me, "Get your car off my skid marks! What are you doing? Back up! You're ruining my evidence!" I was first puzzled as to why he thought my car would somehow erase them. My second question was how exactly he was going to collect them and put them into evidence. Our policy in a situation like that doesn't require us to even photograph the skid marks as part of our investigation. Realizing he was being ridiculous, I just laughed and left him to his mess.

This same guy was with me for an out-of-control juvenile one night. She was positively the snottiest, nastiest little girl I had ever met. She was a little thing, but what she lacked in stature she made up for with attitude. Mom was scared to exact physical discipline, but I told her to go right ahead, and informed the stepdad that he could assist as well.

I had handled the call to my satisfaction and was just about to leave when old screamer had enough of this little girl and he yelled at the mother, "Does she have a radio in her room?" Mom affirmed. He snapped at the mom, "Well, take it out of her room. Go do it now before I leave." Then he snapped, "Does she have a TV in her room?" Mom again affirmed. He told her, "Take that out too, now, while I'm standing here."

"Those are merely suggestions," I butted in, trying to rectify the fact that we cannot give orders to that effect. This cop then said the strangest thing I have ever heard: "If your daughter gets in your face again, knock her out.

Now you'll catch a case for that, but don't worry, you won't lose your job."

It took me a moment to process that he just told this woman to knock her kid out, which would result in her arrest for child abuse—but not to worry because she wouldn't lose her job. Needless to say, this was not good advice. I had to interrupt.

"Don't knock your daughter out. You can spank her, but knocking her out is not a good idea, and if you do, you will most likely be arrested unless she was coming at you with a knife or something like that. In either case, we can't guarantee what your employer will do." I'm sure the screamer had just been irritated with the girl and lost his temper, but still, no excuses.

Now for the finale of stupid stories—mine! I was working with a cop who irritated me more than anyone else. It was two of the longest and worst weeks of my career. Imagine being stuck in a car with someone for ten hours a day you can't stand the sight of. We were called to help an officer who had two people under arrest. We took one of the arrestees and put him in our car; the cop we were helping took the other. It was decided we were to wait for the tow truck to come to take the criminal's car to the pound.

My partner, our prisoner, and I waited for the tow while the other cop left with his prisoner to go start all the paperwork. Our prisoner sat patiently in the back seat where only a Plexiglas window separated us. In the middle of the barrier is a small window just large enough for someone to stick their head through to be able to talk to people in the back seat.

We were there for almost an hour waiting for the tow, and our prisoner hadn't said a word or made a sound. The tow truck came, took the car away, and I started to drive around again. I hadn't gone three blocks when a robbery came out in our district. I quickly put on the lights and siren and began to go try to save the day. My partner began trying to tell me something, but we were far enough into our two weeks that I had just had enough.

"Shut up. I'm driving," I said. "You keep your fucking mouth shut tonight. Just sit there. I've had it with you. If you say one more fucking word, I'll shove you out of this car and you can walk back to the station!"

I went to the robbery and made it all the way there. I extinguished the headlights and was driving slowly, looking for the robber. Something caught my eye.

As I turned to see what it was, I noticed our prisoner, still in handcuffs, sitting as far forward as he could, helping us look for the robber. His head was almost poking through the center window of the Plexiglas. When I looked at him, he shot me a look like, "Don't look at me, look for the robber." He was trying to help search with all the effort he could muster. I had completely forgotten he was in the back seat. I had goofed big time, endangering a handcuffed prisoner by bringing him on a robbery call. I tried to play it off like I knew what I was doing, but then I took responsibility. I was embarrassed about my mistake and I made up with my officer partner because had I not been such a jerk and listened to him, it never would have happened.

Officers are held to a higher standard and punished on multiple fronts when we make mistakes. We have to answer to the courts, the department, and the community. This is exactly this type of accountability that keeps the position of police officer in check.

It's important to remember, however, that we aren't robots. Police make mistakes. It's the officer's obligation to do the right thing and take responsibility as soon as we realize we've made an error. I ask the citizens to have some compassion and understanding that we are only human.

17
WILL THE DEFENDANT PLEASE RISE

Part of an officer's job is to regularly go to court. It's a tedious, arduous process that usually occurs on our day off early in the morning. Thankfully, we are allowed to put ourselves on call most of the time, so the prosecutors only call when needed. If called, we have one hour to show up at the courthouse. This on-call process isn't allowed for certain types of hearings, and for the life of me I can't figure out why. Officer's attendance is required in every single traffic case or motion hearing. It's a stupid policy because these two cases are dismissed, plea-bargained, or continued as often as any other type of case we attend. For all the arrests a big city street cop makes, it's rare a case goes to trial and cops are required to testify. Thankfully, a supermajority of cases are plea-bargained.

I hate court more than anything. When on call, the attorneys will usually phone and in a panic say, "This thing is going. We're going to need you. How fast can you get down here? An hour you say? Can you be down here any sooner?" I rush and get down there, check in and then wait in the hall where I'm told, "Don't go anywhere. You are going to be called any moment." I'm too scared to even go to the bathroom, and then I sit there for hours and hours waiting. My fear is always that a warrant will be issued for my arrest because I tried to sneak away to the bathroom right as they call me to testify.

One time I sat there for eight hours only to be told they weren't going to use me. This was after the call to my house at 8:00 in the morning, "Get down here now. Can you be here in a half hour?" The district attorneys and city attorneys try to be considerate, but they don't really do a good job. Most of the judges are even worse. They let the cops sit there, sometimes for hours, before calling the case where a defendant isn't even present, only to issue a bench warrant and then tell the cop, "You can go home." I always walk out of there mumbling, "You couldn't have done that an hour ago?"

A buddy and I were pushing our luck skiing about an hour and a half away from the city. His cell phone rang while on the chairlift and they told him they needed him immediately. Since he had driven, my day was shot now too. We got down the mountain, raced back to town where he got changed, and got to court as quickly as we could. When he walked in, he found out the district attorneys changed their mind a while ago and didn't need him to testify. They actually forgot he was coming and when he walked in, they asked, "What are you doing here?" He reminded them which trial he was called in for, to which they replied, "Oh, that got continued."

If testifying is actually needed, credibility is called into question and the poor cop is grilled by defense attorneys over the smallest points of what happened. Defense attorneys usually don't call cops liars, but instead condescendingly say, "Maybe you don't recall correctly what happened."

Keep in mind, by the time a case goes to court it has usually been over a year since the event. Also, as cops we respond to several of these types of events per day. Despite the fact every case is unique, it's difficult not to have them blend together sometimes. And no matter how well documented everything is on the scene of a crime, there is undoubtedly something else a prosecutor wishes would have been written down. The next time I'm on a similar scene, I usually remember to document the answer to the question we missed previously. Undoubtedly it's a moot point for the new case and there was something else that didn't get asked or documented.

People have to be asked tons of questions on the scene a crime. These statements have to be in writing to cover what happened, so it's impossible to ask everything. It's just an imperfect system; it always has been and always will be.

On the scene of a shooting, for example, there are just too many things to document. If everything was documented, it would be a book for what every person saw. How far away were they from the actual shooting? Was that distance measured? What was said? What was done? How many shots were heard? What did the shooters look like? Those are all relatively simple and usually get asked.

Questions can start to get so detailed that it is impossible to ask all of them. What type of shirt did he have on? What color were the stripes? Were they horizontal or vertical? Was the shirt tucked in or pulled out? How long was the shirt? Was it short-sleeved or long-sleeved? Did it have a collar on it? What brand was it? Did it have any writing on the front or back? What color was the writing? That's just for the shirt. Imagine doing that for all aspects of a crime scene: each suspect, the victim, the gun, every piece of evidence, the getaway car, etc. Undoubtedly, there are going to be questions that don't get asked. Those so-called mistakes are exploited in trials to make the cop look like an imbecile who can't tie his own shoes without drooling. I would rather go to the dentist and have a cavity filled than go to court. At least then there is cause for drooling on myself.

If all of that goes well and the defendant is found guilty, judges give these people way too many chances when sentencing them. I actually heard a judge say one time, "Mister So-and-So, this is your sixth time violating the restraining order against your wife. I am sentencing you to four years in the state correctional facility, which I will suspend on the condition that you complete the required classes." Yeah, I'm sure he learned his lesson.

That was bad, but if I've seen anything in court that makes me want to turn in my badge and go pick up trash, it was this little fiasco. A woman we were investigating for neglecting her kids had punched a fellow cop in the chest. It wasn't a hard punch, and he was wearing a bulletproof vest with a trauma plate so it couldn't have hurt. It was a weak little sissy punch, but nonetheless, it was flagrant and intentional, and people shouldn't ever be allowed to punch a cop.

I can't remember why it was we were dealing with her. I believe her child was found wandering around in the street. No charges ever came of the alleged child neglect. The kid had just wandered off, wasn't endangered, and hadn't been gone that long. It wasn't as if the child was out for hours, unnoticed by any parent or guardian.

We charged her with a simple assault for the punch to the officer. When the case went to court, the judge accepted a deal. The woman pled guilty, as per the agreement. The judge gave her thirty days in jail, which was suspended on the condition this woman not get in any more trouble for a year. Also assessed was a $200 fine, all of which was suspended on the same condition. Then there was $20 in court costs that the woman had to pay.

I don't know about you, but when getting a parking ticket for expired license plates is *$55 more* than hitting a cop in the chest, something is wrong with the system. I wanted more than anything to stand up and yell to this judge, "What the hell is wrong with you? Twenty bucks for punching a cop in the chest? Are you nuts?" I'm sure my fine would have been more than $20 for that little outburst. Ironic, isn't it?

There are some highlights going to court, albeit they are few and far between. Undoubtedly, there is nothing more hilarious than watching someone act as their own lawyer without a law degree. I get a kick out of this. I might be willing to go to court more often if guaranteed some of this action. People watch entirely too much television. They believe they are Matlock. They scream things like, "Isn't it true…" and "I object…" and "I have nothing further for this witness, he may be excused." Hilarious.

In traffic court, if it isn't a designated criminal violation (something serious), there is no prosecutor. Say for instance you are going to court to fight a stop sign ticket. In that instance, it would just be you, the cop, and the judge. The cop goes first. So I would get up there and establish all the necessary elements. Then when I'm done, the judge asks you if you have any questions for me. I have yet to see anyone ask a real question. Instead, people use this opportunity to start to testify. The judge will stop the testimony, point out that no question is being asked, and then say, "You are testifying. You will have your chance to testify in a moment. Right now, all you should be doing is asking questions about what the officer has said. Now please continue." Nobody ever listens to this. They say, "Okay," and then start testifying again. I sit there while the judge's admonishments get louder and sterner and try not to laugh.

When that painful process is all over, they testify. This is when—and I'm completely serious—people usually tell a lie they believe makes the whole thing legal, but what they really do is admit to the crime. They will say something like, "I saw the officer, and I stopped after the sign so he would be sure to see my tires stop." This is still illegal because in most states cars are required to stop before the stop line or crosswalk, whichever is present.

Another one people like to try quite often is, "The person in front of me didn't stop either and they didn't get pulled over." Then, when the judge hands out the sentence—and this is the best part—they get the full point assessment against their license, no plea bargain. This is where people then try to accept the plea agreement offered to them before they lost. Hysterical.

The best self-representation was an idiot I stopped for driving under the influence. I was transporting a prisoner to headquarters, driving down the highway and I saw a car literally going about thirty-five miles per hour, swerving from side to side, almost striking the walls on either side of the highway. I had never made a traffic stop with a prisoner before, as it's not allowed, unless it is a life and death situation. This is because if my police car gets rear-ended on the highway while the prisoner is in back, I'm responsible. It's also possible I could get in a fight or a shootout with the driver of the car and my poor prisoner would be relegated to front-row seating. If my prisoner gets hurt, it's my responsibility.

Other cars were pulling alongside me and pointing out the weaving car. Everyone was afraid to pass the guy. The other drivers were holding up their arms like, "Aren't you going to do anything?" Finally, I had to stop the guy myself as I couldn't get anyone else there fast enough. Allowing him to continue on until another officer arrived was too dangerous.

After he pulled over, I called for a backup unit before I approached the car. I wanted the backup unit to watch my prisoner (and me, for that matter). After backup got there, I finally went up to the car, irritated at the fact that I now had a DUI to process on top of my first arrest paperwork, both of which would take me hours to finish. I wasn't quite sure how I was going to do it all before the end of shift.

The guy rolled down his window and I only said, "Get out of the car." He did get out, but refused everything else. No roadsides, no breath or blood test, and no interview. He was completely wasted, and a drunk, belligerent asshole. He reeked of booze and he was swearing and yelling and calling me names the whole night.

There is nothing I hate more than dealing with drunk people. They ask the same questions over and over, they don't understand anything, they pee on themselves, they spit, swear, vomit, fall over, and smell, and are basically a pain in the ass. A specialized DUI officer helped me process this particular guy, thank goodness. She also managed to take a photo of him while he was flipping us off, complete with his bloodshot eyes and disheveled clothes.

Since this wasn't a stop sign violation but a criminal DUI case, there was a prosecuting attorney and the defendant was also entitled to an attorney or to have one appointed for him if he could not afford one. Instead, he decided to pass on any attorneys and represent himself.

I got up and answered questions from the prosecution detailing all of what happened, including how rare it was to have to make a stop with a prisoner aboard. I detailed why I didn't go up to the car until backup arrived. I went on to talk about what was said between us, what I observed, and so on and so forth.

Soon, it was this guy's chance to cross-examine me. He got up, swaggered around in his jeans, and sauntered about like he was pondering his glorious strategy. He finally spoke, and in a stern, no-nonsense tone he dramatically yelled, "Isn't it true, Officer, that after you pulled me over, you didn't come up to the car for a long time?"

I agreed and again explained why that was. He then asked me, "And isn't it true, Officer, that when you came up to my window, you didn't ask for my driver's license, registration, or insurance; instead you just told me to 'get out of the car'?" I again agreed.

The man sauntered around a minute like he had me just where he wanted me. I thought he was about to unleash the wrath of his third-grade education when he spun quickly and said, "I have nothing further, your honor. This witness may step down."

He was found guilty—imagine that. I'm sure the jury getting a look at the photograph sealed our case. Too bad this whole thing wasn't on TV. The ratings would have been through the roof. The reason it wasn't televised, I'm convinced, is because I would've had to be on the show, and as everyone knows, when a cop winds up on television, it usually isn't good.

18
LIGHTS, CAMERA, ACTION

There are few people in this word except reality TV stars who can go from nobodies to celebrities in one day, and for those, the attention is usually positive. The media would rather report on bad cops than the heroes. Most of us can't recall the names of cops killed in the line of duty. We do remember the names of officers who get in trouble. Sergeant Stacey Koon is famous for the Rodney King beating. Detective Mark Furman is famous, not for his work as a detective, but for being caught on tape saying a racial slur. Cops know we are only one second away from infamy.

I have an unusual perspective on this because I have worked in the media for several years. I worked at two television stations as a producer. For a while, I was a radio traffic reporter, and then a news anchor on a big radio station. After that, for several years I had my own talk show on Denver's biggest AM station 850 KOA. I had to give up the show when I was promoted to sergeant because my seniority reset and I couldn't get the weekend off. My show wasn't just about police issues. I talked about all kinds of current events. What I brought to the table, however, was the perspective of a cop. This perspective about the world and how it works is helpful in all different kinds of situations and topics. Because of my work as a police officer, for sure, I am more assertive than before. Also, I can listen—and I mean really listen—to someone, a trait that is slowly moving toward extinction.

I understand the media. I know how they work and how they think. I know how tough it is to tell a story in thirty seconds. A radio talk-show is one of the only exceptions to this, which is why I am so fond of that format. As a host, I can spend an hour on a topic and present multiple sides. I can tell more of the facts that don't make the cut on the evening news. Every media outlet has an agenda. The good news about my show was that it was not intended to be unbiased. It's radio's equivalent to an op-ed piece.

The rest of the media has made news and information quick, fast, and convenient for us. They tell us what is happening in the world all in neat little packages of a few seconds. The news used to do a better job in reporting, and now I only use it as a suggested study guide. I hear the ongoing stories, decide which ones interest me, and then research them on my own.

The mainstream media's problem is that there are few stories that can be told from all sides in such a short time, especially cop stories. To understand a news story involving a police officer, the circumstances and information given to the officer before the events need to be known. The training of the officer and the procedures of the department are essential to know in order to understand why a cop acted in a certain way. To be completely fair, the cop's account of what happened, what was observed, and what was said also need to be made public. Police departments have put together shoot boards, review committees, and layers upon layers of other types of oversight. Then, when there's a controversial shooting and the community is outraged, they cry foul after only hearing a fraction of the account. The media picks whatever headlines they think will get ratings. The more controversial the story, the better the ratings and the more money they make.

The department's goal is to get convictions in court. Information comes in quickly at first and much of it proves to be false or different than we originally thought. How would it look in court if we put out information that turned out to be incorrect? If we went to a scene that appeared to be a suicide and came out telling the media, "Yup, it's a suicide," only to later find out that this person was murdered and it was made to look like a suicide, it would be much tougher to get a conviction. Lawyers would tell jurors their client was innocent and then play the clip of us telling the world it's a suicide.

We are also very limited in what information we can release following an incident. We cannot put out information only people involved in the case know. If someone gets shot and killed, who is the only person who knows what kind of gun was used? The person who did it. If the evening news tells the whole world it was a .45-caliber handgun, then when the suspect recants their confession at trial, it will be more difficult to prove their guilt.

After a big incident, we usually hear the most from a family member or friend of the criminal telling us how perfect and upstanding this person was before the police shot him dead for no reason. The department releases very little information. We don't get to hear from the officers involved either.

People think they have heard enough to decide, but remember, things may not always be as they seem at first glance. By the time all the layers of departmental review confirm everything was done within policy, procedure, and the law, it's too late to appease an irate city that decided long ago the cops in their community are all crooked.

In incidents where a cop has to use deadly force or the officer's actions are going to be looked at criminally, why doesn't the officer just come out in the beginning and tell their side of the story? Cops have to answer to a lot of people for their actions. Everything we do is examined by the district attorney or a grand jury for criminal charges, by the department for procedural violations, and attorneys bringing civil suits. A department's review can consist of many different boards and other types of court hearings.

Every department is different in this respect. Mine, for instance, has the Internal Affairs Bureau. Cops investigating other cops—how righteous could that be? Very. I worked in Internal Affairs and they don't just investigate the allegation portion of an incident; they also look at things that weren't even alleged.

For instance, if an officer gets a discourtesy complaint while working in an off-duty police capacity for another entity, one of IAB's first questions is "Did the officer get proper approval to work there?" I can't count the number of times the allegation against the officer was found false or unfounded, yet another unrelated even minor policy violation was discovered and then sustained.

Also in my former department is the Monitor's Office. They are a civilian oversight board that has access to investigations, crime scenes, interviews, and most every other aspect of a case. There doesn't necessarily have to even be an allegation of wrongdoing for the Monitor's Office to get involved.

Departments across the nation have and utilize Use of Force Boards, Tactic Review Boards, Disciplinary Review Boards, Chief's Hearings, Citizen Oversight Boards, and other types of review panels. Some may be disciplinary related, some may evaluate and identify tactics and training issues. In my city, we had several of these boards on top of the others I listed not to mention the Civil Service Commission, yet another civilian entity, that also gets involved in discipline. There are plenty of cooks in the kitchen.

Civil lawsuits can drag on for years, and criminal charges can bankrupt a police officer if he has to pay for his own attorneys. There is enough accountability, enough people to answer to without trying to talk to the media, who will chop up what is said and use it to make the police look as bad as possible.

Misconduct among police officers sells papers and makes ratings soar. Cops know they won't be given long enough to say what needs to be said, and don't trust the media to put it all out there even if they did. "If it bleeds it leads," the old media saying goes.

When there is a controversial police story in town, the media has to interview someone—and who is it, do you suppose, who's willing to talk? It's the outspoken minority made up of cop-haters or people who have something to gain. It's the suspect's family who has their eye on a settlement. It's the community activists who are concerned more with increasing their name recognition and power base than they are about the people involved.

Talk about agendas—*these* people have the biggest out of everyone. They are the racists, of all types, who divide the community with their hate speech. Cops get their name and reputation dragged through the mud, all so everyone else can gain from what's happened. The activists get more power in the community, and the media gets their ratings.

In my city, there was a shooting of an unarmed man. The officers were responding to a domestic call when another man in the house was in bed, and cops ordered him to freeze when he pulled out a shiny pop can from underneath the covers. Thinking the pop can was a gun, one officer shot and killed the man.

Those of you who want to know why the cops don't shoot items out of people's hands really need an explanation. (This is one of the questions I answer most often.) Do you know how hard that would be? The goal of using deadly physical force is to stop the threat. The highest probability of stopping a threat is to hit them in the area of the greatest mass that has the highest chance of stopping the current or imminent assault. That area is in the chest or head. Arms and legs are not only skinny, but they move in all directions as compared to a mid section, which is relatively immobile. People shot in the arm or leg can oftentimes still carry out their assault. A chest can turn side to side, but it still makes for a large target and carries a high probability of stopping the person from their actions. The head is more difficult to hit but has less mobility than arms and legs and the highest probability of stopping a person.

The cop who shot the man didn't have a history of similar incidents and had been on the job many years.

The community was outraged. How could this murderer not be fired, locked up in jail, and the key thrown away? The law, and appropriately so, doesn't criticize like people do. The law takes into account the imperfections of the human psyche. The law only requires that an officer convince a jury he was acting reasonably in deciding that there was an imminent threat against his life. If it was reasonable to believe that, the resulting actions are also appropriate. My city had about seven unarmed shootings in a twenty-seven year period.

Shootings of unarmed suspects will always be a reality in every police department, every city, and in every town. When they occur, depending on the situation and the officer's background and history, it shouldn't result in firing. You can't give an employee training and trust, tell him or her to go out and do their best, and then punish them when they were acting in good faith and their actions were reasonable. Things evolve so quickly it is impossible to be one hundred percent accurate every time.

It would be nice if police could achieve perfection. It would be nice if police never perceived a threat that wasn't actually there. It would also be nice if I were taller. Seven police shootings in twenty-seven years is remarkable, not perfect, but pretty darn good. By my calculations, and because we received over a million calls a year, there is still way less than a one percent chance of this happening.

Once again, people use transference in these instances. Even if you were in a predicament where the cops were telling you to do something, you would do it. I'm pretty sure the last thing any thinking, rational person would do is whip out a shiny pop can from underneath a mattress when told not to move. The man didn't listen to the officer's commands and made a sudden move in the dark while holding something shiny. The officer has to decide in a split second. If we waited until fired upon, there would be many more funerals for the men and women in blue, and the community shouldn't expect their cops to be shot before shooting. It's an officer's job to serve and protect, not to be a sacrificial lamb for people who are intent on hurting others. Nevertheless, I've talked to people on my radio show who believe it is an officer's job to die instead of taking a life.

Natural cop haters—and I've met plenty of them— think we are just itching to blow someone away. These are people I believe have a natural resistance to authority. I haven't ever shot anyone or been in a shooting, so I can't talk about this personally. I'm sure it would make for a more enriching experience if I could enlighten you as to what it was like, but I'm glad I can't.

I can't imagine having to shoot someone, then having it replay constantly in my head. I believe I could do whatever needed to keep myself and others alive. I also believe that I couldn't just come home after shooting someone, pop on the tube, have a beer, and pass out watching reruns of *The Golden Girls* (it's a gay thing).

I've known cops who have been in shootings and seen them right after it happened. They were horribly shaken up. They had the same glazed-over look as a victim who has just been seriously violated, as if they were trying to convince themselves that everything was fine. One of them was only repeating over and over, "Why did he have to do that?" I have yet to see anyone blow the smoke away from the barrel of their gun, smile, and carve another notch in their belt.

There *are* cops who screw up. As with every profession, there are a few bad apples. From what I've seen, they get weeded out, even if it sometimes takes longer than it should. Cops, believe it or not, pay dearly for their mistakes. If a cop is charged criminally, they usually don't get the same plea bargain opportunities John Q. Taxpayer would get because of the perception of unfairness or favoritism. Civil lawyers will take cases against cops that wouldn't normally stand a chance, but they know the city will settle rather than litigate. Try to get a home loan when you are the subject of civil litigation. Nobody wants to lend a person money who might have a judgment coming against them.

I was in an accident that I didn't think was my fault. I rear-ended someone, and as I tell people on every rear-end accident I investigate, "Pretty much if you hit someone from behind, you're at fault." In my case however, a prisoner slipped her handcuffs around front, undid her seatbelt, reached through the cage into the front of the car, and was fighting with me while I went down the highway. I managed only to hit a Ford Ranger at about five miles an hour, knocking the grill of my police car loose. There was no damage to the truck. I thought that was pretty good considering what had happened, but the deputy chief at my hearing after I told my story only said, "Son, in the middle of the word 'life' is the word 'if' and that's what you have to ask yourself: 'What if?'" I still don't know what that means. I wanted to say, "And in the middle of the word 'shit' is the word 'hi.' So, hi-dee-ho, you fuck face." It didn't matter. To him I was at fault, and that was all that counted.

All my friends told me how great it was I didn't get a ticket for the accident. "Wow. So you guys don't even get tickets when you crash into someone? Must be nice!"

Nope. No tickets. Instead, I got a fine day off (which is a day's pay or about $250), eight hours of remedial driving at the academy, eight points off my department driver's license, and a written reprimand that went in my permanent file, which subsequently affected my year-end evaluation. Granted, that was my second crash, but I'd rather have had the four-point ticket on my state driver's license, plea bargained it to two points (a standard court practice), and paid about $150 in fines and court costs. Luckily I wasn't sued by the guy I rear-ended for mental anguish.

When there is any investigation into the actions of police officers, be it criminal or just within the department, the involved officer is the last to be interviewed. Instead, a letter is sent at the beginning of the process to the officer so that he or she can worry about it for the next few months while the wheels of justice turn. Internal Affairs interviews everyone involved, and then, if it is a criminal matter, asks the district attorney whether or not they are going to file charges. If there are no charges, the officer gets an advisement, similar to Miranda, which compels us to give a statement or face termination.

Good cops break the rules and policy all the time. Yes, that's right. Why is that okay, you ask? I'm sure you've seen it: a red light, a cop pulls up to it, turns his lights on, goes through the light, and then turns his lights off. Everyone thinks there's a sale at the doughnut shop, but that's not the case. If I'm on patrol, at work, and not on a call, why would I run a red light when I'm just driving around? All I'm doing is driving in circles. I'm not in a hurry to go anywhere. I don't just drive around in circles code 10. We aren't allowed to run code 10 to many things. Take domestics, for example. The average one is not a code 10 run unless it is with weapons or some other extenuating circumstances exist.

If it were my sister in a fight with her boyfriend I wouldn't want the cop to sit at the red light at 3:00 in the morning and wait even though no other cars are around. I would say, "Hurry up, fucker." So we do. And guess who will be getting the "life" speech if they wreck going through an intersection on a call they aren't supposed to have their lights on for? Our intentions are usually good, but people assume the worst.

Other times when we are going code 10, we have to shut the siren down when we get close to the call so as to not say to the bad guy, "We're almost here. Run now or take hostages." Sometimes we shut down all the equipment but we may still have an intersection or two to get through before we arrive to the call. So, we turn on the lights only to warn other motorists, get through the intersection, and turn them off again. Guess who gets in trouble if they wreck while only having their lights on and not their siren, even if a code 10 run is justified? The reality is that we all do things we shouldn't to help people, but I would do them any day if it has a chance to stop someone from getting hurt.

People are always questioning the actions of cops. If cops are gathered in a group at the 7-11, everyone assumes they are goofing off and not working. When, in reality, we meet at the 7-11, not just to goof off, but to make plans about pickups on warrants or other police setups we may be doing that night.

One time I was forced to wait in the parking lot of a grocery store for over three hours. The Metro-Gang Task Force was watching a drug house where a stolen car was in the driveway. They were hoping someone would come get in the car and drive away so at the bare minimum, there would be an arrest for auto theft. The whole time I was trapped in this lot, I would give anything to be able to leave. I'm sure people saw me sitting there for hours on end and thought I was waiting for a fresh shipment of Krispy Kreme doughnuts to arrive. Don't get me wrong—sometimes cops meet just to have some coffee, an occasional doughnut, and tell stories, and that's okay too.

On vacation one year, some stupid friend of a friend saw some cops in a parking lot and said, "Why are cops always trying to dig up trouble when it's quiet? They are always looking to beat someone up or get in a fight."

First of all, his premise is that cops are inherently violent. I've already discussed how sometimes violence is a necessary evil and part of the job. In this guy's world, people are all good, and they don't hurt one another. Everyone can be reasoned with or convinced to do the right thing.

Secondly, I would hope all of you as taxpayers would want cops out stirring up trouble when it's quiet. After all, that's what you pay us for. It's during those times when the gun-carrying drug dealers get pulled over, and good, self-initiated arrests make the entire community safer. When it's quiet and calls aren't coming out, we can finally set up on the parking lot where car break-ins have been occurring.

Two of us were hiding on the roof of an apartment building one night that was having a lot of drug activity and break-ins. We were up there for a while because no calls were coming out. This was a small complex, gated with long iron bars. There was a "no trespass order" for the property, which means, "If you don't live here, you can't be here."

We were sitting there waiting for something to happen when something did. Two guys climbed over the fence. They were sitting there obviously hatching some sort of plan when we came down to talk to them. They had no good explanation for and couldn't seem to agree on why they were there, where they had come from, or what it was they were doing.

We patted them down for weapons. I took one, and my partner took the other. I was chatting with my suspect as I checked him for weapons. I had known the other cop for a while. He was a cool cat and very calm. When I looked up at him halfway through his search, his face was completely white and he had his gun in his suspect's back. I heard him say to the guy he was searching, "Don't move or I will shoot you. Now, I want you to go down to your knees very slowly." I pulled out my gun and kept it on both suspects.

If my level-headed partner was this scared, something must have been really wrong. He reached into this kid's waistband and pulled out an uzi, and I mean just like you would see in the movies, complete with a long banana clip.

It turns out that this kid had a ton of crack cocaine on him. It was more crack than I had ever seen in my life. Later as we counted it, I was reminded of the movie *Training Day*, where with each rock of crack we counted, we were also counting out the resulting prison years. He was tried federally and was sentenced to about fifteen years in the penitentiary. Then again, maybe we shouldn't have been stirring up trouble when things weren't busy.

I wish we all could get along and no violence was necessary. Believe it or not, most police officers are not the kids who had their lunch money taken when they were young. Most of us are hardworking, gentle, caring, giving, sacrificing people who would give our lives for a complete stranger. Sometimes that's worthy of some recognition.

19
THE RIPPLE EFFECT

I wish it were the heroic things that replay in my mind; however, it's usually the trauma and horrific events I've seen that give me flashbacks. Sometimes a gory scene bothers me more than others. I once responded to a suicide where a man went into his bedroom, put a revolver in his mouth, and blew his head wide open. The wife and children came running in to see what the noise was and found their husband and father with his brains splattered everywhere. They were all sobbing and surely traumatized for life. The image of that man lying on the bed and the looks on the faces of his family still appear in my head sometimes when I close my eyes.

The only plus side to all my crazy experiences is that when I go out with friends, I am the man with the stories. I tell my tales to gawks of, "Ooooh" and "Aaaaah!" And while it's nice to be the one everyone looks at and wonders how I do the job of a police officer every day, those things I can't shake off are the worst. For the most part, I just go on, because I have to.

For those things that have stuck with me forever, I find myself thinking about the grief, the family, and the loss. The memory is reignited if I even get near the physical area where it occurred. I drive the streets of Denver thinking, "That corner is where that guy got shot, oh and that block is where that fire happened."

Even years later when I'm in a neighborhood or district I used to work, these memories pop in my head as I pass different intersections, buildings, or streets. Sometimes a scene with human trauma is bothersome, but many times it's the small things that bother me. I may not even see the guts and gore, but someone, or something that was said, or the look on a face can haunt me for a long time.

It's not just the effect all this has had on me. There are compounding effects from all these crimes. It's not just the victim and suspect. It's not just an assault or a burglary. The lives of many people are altered forever with each crime. This is what I try never to think about. It saddens me a great deal to think about all of the ripple effects each crime has throughout the families, neighborhoods, communities and even generations of people to come.

Earlier, I shared how many of the sex assault cases I investigated turned out to be false allegations. For the ones that were real, I would go through all of the other bogus cases just to help those victims. These cases are also very difficult to hear and deal with. These women have to be questioned about everything that happened. Where did he put his penis? Was he wearing a condom? Did he ejaculate and if so, where? These are all things we need to know in order to retrieve evidence. I still don't know how to ask these questions and feel good about them. These are very difficult things to ask a woman who's just been raped. They are private, embarrassing, and make the victim have to remember the details of the event over and over.

There is a very real trauma on the victims' faces. It's almost as if nobody is home. Those are the faces that haunt me and keep me up late at night. I spent as much time as I could with these people. Driving them to the hospital while they sat up front in my car, telling them it would be okay, and most importantly, explaining what was happening every step of the way.

One girl in particular stands out in my mind. She was dating an older boy, much to the chagrin of her mother. The girl had slipped out her window to be with her boyfriend at his house. He made advances toward her, and had brutally raped her after she told him no. She had come home, put her blood-stained clothes in the hamper, changed into new clothes, and after a while, got into the shower with the new clothes still on. She was sitting in there, fully clothed, crying, and bleeding from her vagina when her mother found her.

As soon as I got there, I knew this was for real. When I talked to her she was shaking and could barely speak. I could hear the beginnings of what was going to be her blaming herself while she talked on and on about the different "should haves" and "could haves." It was a painful day for everyone. At least the boyfriend was arrested.

It was her uncontrollable shaking and her glassy, blank stare that haunted me after this particular call. I imagined what it would be like for her future husband. Would she ever get past this? Would they ever have a healthy intimate relationship because of what happened? Would her kids suffer as she would be overprotective and try to guard them against the evil she experienced?

It was undeniable that this girl's life had been forever altered. I imagined all the little things that would never be the same in her life, little things she might not even attribute to the sex assault. Maybe she would have a deep hatred toward men, and never have a healthy relationship. Maybe she wouldn't go out at night. It's hard to know what something like that really does to a person. It's better not to imagine the possibilities.

What about the suspect? While most people will be happy to see the rapist behind bars, what about his parents? Having your son in jail for rape can't be easy to live with. It's likely hard for anyone that interacted with him on a daily basis. His friends, neighbors, employer, coworkers…everyone will feel the ripple of consequences from his actions.

It isn't just sex assaults. Moments of rage, passion, and fear can change lives forever.

I went to the stabbing of a seventeen-year-old boy at an inner-city high school. The suspect was a sixteen-year-old classmate. It wasn't gang related. I didn't see the body, just a couple of specks of blood on the ground. I didn't have to ride down in the ambulance with the victim where attendants would cut off all his bloody clothing. I didn't have to watch the paramedic speeding his way to the emergency room in a race against time destined to fail. I didn't even get to see the murder weapon. I didn't have to see any of those things this time. Instead, my only job was to transport two witnesses to headquarters so detectives could interview them.

I tried to put things at ease and act like a "cool guy" so they would relax. It seemed to work. Once at headquarters, all I had to do was sit at the end of a long bland hallway and watch three separate doorways to assure that none of the witnesses left or talked to one another. It was that simple. After I was relieved, I found my way to the little room where a bunch of detectives were sitting around watching the interview of the suspect unfold on a television screen.

The interview room was plain, only a clock and paper calendar on the walls. The sixteen-year-old suspect and his mother and father sat at the table, answering questions for the detective and one of the deputy district attorneys. The family didn't yet know the fate of the young man who was stabbed. During the questioning, the father would periodically ask in a desperate tone if the other boy was all right.

Watching the interview, I came to learn how the whole thing started. The two boys had bumped into each other in the hall earlier in the day and dirty looks were exchanged. Later, in the lunchroom, the two began to fight. One boy was getting beaten up pretty badly when he took a small, serrated knife from a sheath he had made at home and stabbed the other boy in the heart two times. A third stab wound was at the boy's liver. The victim ran off and so did the suspect. The victim didn't get far before he stopped and collapsed.

I continued to watch the interview and hear the suspect tell the detectives he was only defending himself. I watched the father agree with his son, who had run to the grocery store and called his dad after the attack. The mom met up with them and they all three turned themselves in to the police as a family.

At the very end of the interview, detectives told the family, "I'm sorry to have to tell you this, but the other boy passed away a short time ago at the hospital."

I watched the mother double over with what looked like unbearable pain in her abdomen. I watched the father cry and pull his son's head close to his body and rock back and forth, telling him between sobs, "I know you didn't mean to kill him," over and over again.

Then, I looked at the boy. He cried so hard it looked as if he was having a seizure. His sobs were audible not just from the speakers on the TV monitor, but echoed simultaneously from the interview room down the hall.

I watched as a family was torn apart. That moment, they realized they had lost each other. It wasn't just the murdered boy whose life was ruined—it was all of his family, friends, neighbors, and acquaintances. What about the one going to jail? Now his life was ruined too, along with that of his parents, grandparents, friends, and neighbors.

It was also the now-altered lives of several witnesses, all just children, who watched their classmate and friend get stabbed to death in the place they call school. It was at that moment that I realized the real pain is in the aftermath. It's all of the sleepless nights, the thoughts that something could have been done to stop all of this pain that haunts everyone, right down to the lowly policeman whose only job was to transport the witnesses to headquarters.

When the media reported this crime, I thought about how parents around the city would be more frightened sending their children off to school each day. I thought about the police officers who would be assigned and security guards who would be hired to work at the school in attempt to make everyone feel safe and to reduce the chances of something like this happening again. Other schools would follow suit hoping to prevent similar incidents.

Even future kids bringing their new pocketknives to school would be treated differently. Penalties would be more stiff and citations would be issued. New rules, regulations, and laws would be drafted to address this growing danger.

These are some of the more difficult things I have had to process. Even now, while thinking about them, they make me incredibly sad. I have to fight back tears while the flashbacks come and go. I did this job in hopes that my actions prevented some of this from happening or at least held people accountable when they did. Your police officers are still out there every day making one of these two things happen. It's important to recognize their efforts and encourage them to continue to do their best to accomplish this goal.

20
AND THE AWARD GOES TO...

The nature of police work is that we are asked to respond to an incident and put our own lives in jeopardy to help a complete stranger. I did it every day for over fifteen years. I am proud of the fact that I was the one you called at 2:00 in the morning when someone had broken into your house and you were locked in the bedroom. I wanted to be the one who drives to your home, comes in, and saves you. It didn't matter your race, religion, political views, sexual orientation, age, gender, or any other factor.

I've had people tell me that they love when an officer gets killed and that they hope we all die. But at 2:00 AM, when a killer breaks into their house, they still call the police, and I was happy to come save them as well.

I see officers save lives all the time. Sometimes, they talk someone off a ledge, or into putting a gun down. Sometimes, they use less than lethal force to disarm someone who is about to hurt themselves or someone else. I've seen officers do first aid and CPR to save a life. Those are the obvious examples.

Then there are the many lives saved that are not so obvious. Times when most people never know that an officer's actions saved a life or prevented a future crime. These instances are harder to recognize, but undoubtedly still exist. For instance, an officer gets in a foot chase with a shooting suspect and catches him. If he had not been caught, he would have murdered someone else before finally being apprehended.

An officer spends time with someone or recommends a resource for someone who is battling depression. The officer is able to get through to the person who would have otherwise committed suicide. An officer develops a rapport with a kid who is getting involved in gangs and is able to change his life. Had the officer not succeeded in making a difference, the youth would have gone on to murder someone.

Obviously, these more obscure instances of life saving cannot be measured and sometimes are never even proven, but they certainly exist. The events that can be proven are the ones for which officers receive awards and recognition. If you have time, attend an awards ceremony for your local law enforcement agency. Most of these ceremonies are incredible. See just how many officers receive awards and listen to what happened. They call up the officers involved, read a narrative about the event, and it's so amazing to hear the stories of bravery, selflessness, courage, love, and compassion these officers have for all mankind. Then for every award and situation you hear about, think about the many that went unrecognized.

A cop I worked with was sitting late one night in a dark parking lot with another officer. They were catching up on their daily activity log and visiting. It was the middle of the night and the calls had slowed down. A van came around the corner quite a distance away, just barely visible to the officers. At a stop sign it appeared to the officers something fell out of the van. The driver got out, put whatever had fallen back inside the van and drove off again. It looked a little curious, but wasn't something that clearly would have caused someone to jump into action.

"What was that a sack of potatoes?" one officer said to the other.

They decided to go check it out and see what was going on. They pulled behind the van as it pulled into the parking space in front of the man's residence. It didn't take long to determine they had made a wise decision. What had fallen out of the van was the man's girlfriend. He had driven an hour south, kidnapped and beat her, and was driving her back to his apartment to kill her. She was totally out of it. It took the officers some time to get her coherent. Later on in the interview, after cooperating with the officers, she thanked them.

"He would have killed me if you didn't help. Thank you so much," she said. I heard about this incident later and those officers never received any formal recognition for that incident.

There were times I received formal recognition for my actions while on the job. I once received a medal for evacuating an apartment building on fire. As we entered the building, the smoke was so thick we had to stay low to the ground to avoid breathing it in. The smoke looked like low-lying fog over a lake, but it was reversed. The smoke was near the ceiling and there was a distinct line where the smoke stopped. The air was very clear near the floor. We worked quickly as we made our way door to door clearing out the residents. I finally made it to the last door and pounded on it.

A female answered the door, panicking. It was a weird sort of panic, however. I could tell she was scared, but she wasn't screaming or running around. It just appeared her brain was misfiring and she wasn't thinking clearly.

"I'm coming, I'm just packing a bag," she explained to me with a blank stare on her face.

"There's no time for that! Leave everything! Come with me now!" My every sentence got more and more urgent.

"Okay, just let me grab a couple things," she said as she turned and walked away from the doorway.

What was this woman thinking? I had a good mind to get the hell out and leave her there.

"Well, I tried!" I would explain to my superiors. I was so angry at that moment. I wanted nothing more than to get out of this building. I went in after her and gently turned her around after grabbing her arm.

"We are going to die if you don't come with me right now!" I sure felt like this was the case.

We got out of the building after crawling down the hallway on our hands and knees. I have never been so thankful to have exited a building.

My sergeant wrote us up after this was over but never mentioned it to any of us. Several months later, we received notice we would be award recipients at the next ceremony. It was my first major award and I was flattered and appreciative for the recognition.

I was also formally recognized for responding to a different apartment building one day on the report of a jumper. When I got there, I discovered a mentally challenged eleven-year-old boy who was on the second story rooftop of an apartment building. His frantic mother was there, telling us about how she couldn't get him to take his psychological medications that day.

I went in to the bedroom and leaned out the window. I started to try to talk to him to see what was going on, but the child appeared to believe he was some sort of animal, acting like a tiger or a lion. I was having zero success with anything I was saying.

The roof was triangle-shaped with a slant on each side, forming a peak in the middle and shingles sloping away from the peak on either side. The roof was fairly wide but the slopes were very steep. It was over twenty feet to the ground.

The fire department had put a ladder up on the south side of the roof and a firefighter was trying to sneak to the top. The boy noticed her and ran toward the peak of the roof. It was at this point I knew I had to do more than talk.

Seeing that the young man was concentrated solely on the firefighter, I got out on the roof. Just as I did, he heard me and turned his attention back to me all the while making his way toward the edge of the roof. We both made eye contact and I saw the whites of his eyes get really big. With that same look, he looked to the ground then back at me. I knew the boy was about to jump off the roof. I was close enough to grab him, so I lunged forward, grabbing his arm. I was able to bring us both inside safely.

My partner wrote this incident up for an award, and I received a medal from my department. I was also recognized by the Denver Optimist Club as an Officer of the Month. I won the Mike Dowd Award at the annual Policeman's Ball, and I was even nominated for a Presidential Medal of Valor for my actions.

I was surprised with the attention I received. I felt honored and humbled by it all. It felt good to be appreciated.

Public opinion, however, seems to be focused on the negative. Many believe officers are out of control nationwide, but it's time for a perspective check.

Police departments handle millions of calls across the country each year. My department took in over a million calls into the communications center annually. And that's just one department. Over the course of a year, only about 300-500 cases come through the Internal Affairs Bureau. Many of those are bogus complaints. But even if every one of those cases turned up wrongdoing on the part of an officer, and that's certainly not the case, that would only be .0005% of the total calls. This doesn't mean we excuse any wrongdoing on the part of an officer when it does happen. It also doesn't mean people who have been victimized by misconduct should be forgotten. Officers should and are held accountable when they make mistakes. More attention should be given to the majority of police actions, which are positive.

Public education is one missing piece and the complexity and time it takes to explain it all is great. If you are truly interested in learning more about the truth and depth of each case, consult with your local district attorney's office.

In my city, unless the case goes to a grand jury, the elected district attorney releases a letter detailing all the facts and circumstances of a case where an officer has shot someone but doesn't face prosecution. The letter is a detailed explanation of why the officer's actions were reasonable. Those letters are still available online for anyone to read. Many cities across the United States do something similar. Find one for a case you remember in the news and read it. See if it doesn't offer a satisfactory explanation as to why the officer's actions were reasonable and prudent.

And while most of the media and our community is focused on the negative, the police are out there the other 99.9995% of the time saving your daughter who was kidnapped and beaten, your mother whose apartment building was on fire, and your son who is about to jump off the roof.

21
TWENTY-ONE GUN SALUTE

No matter what we do for a living, everyone knows that any day could be our last. It could be that we get hit by a bus while crossing the street, we could have a sudden heart attack, a drunk driver could T-bone us at any of the many intersections we cross through each day, and in one second we're dead. This isn't something most people spend a lot of time thinking about. Sure, once in a while we read about some poor family driving down the highway when a bridge dislodges and falls on their car at the exact second they are crossing under it. For a moment, we all say, "Man, that could have been me." But that thought lasts about as long as a prom night sexcapade.

Being a cop, however, begins with a simple and undeniable fact: This could be the last day of my life. Police officers are forced to spend a great deal of time with their own mortality. It starts in the academy where they subject new officers to a string of stories and videos showing cops being killed in the line of duty. I thought about my death every time I dressed for work. I have a wooden rosary that I believe was given to me by an angel.

I was at a particularly difficult time in my life personally. I had arrested this woman for identity theft. She was an illegal immigrant using someone's social security number. But, the day after I arrested her, she posted bond and came to visit me. She thanked me for doing my job, and said she felt I was struggling. She brought me a wooden rosary and a bracelet with the different saints on it. She gave me a hug, told me I was being guarded and protected, and gave me these trinkets to remind me of that every day. I never saw that woman again.

As I got dressed for work every night, it's when I put the rosary on I said, "I hope tonight isn't the night, but if it is, I hope it's fast." Throughout the night, I'd be reminded I was wearing it because when I moved, it often shifted under my ballistic vest, poking me slightly. It's in these moments I remembered how vulnerable I was. I knew even the simplest of calls could snowball out of control in microseconds and I could be dead.

We had an officer who had arrested a juvenile in an alley after witnessing the suspect breaking into cars. He transmitted over the radio that he had the suspect in custody. A few moments later the officer was killed after the juvenile produced a handgun and shot the officer in the chest. His ballistic vest stopped the first few rounds. Then, the boy stood over the officer and shot him twice in his head, killing him. The officer was survived by his expecting wife.

No matter what call I went on, there was always a little voice asking if today could be the day that I'd have to make the ultimate sacrifice. Strangely, I usually wasn't scared during the course of my workday. Things evolved and happened so quickly that most of the time, in the moment, there was no time to be scared. When there was an incident where I could have been seriously hurt or killed, I didn't reflect on that fact until after everything was over. It was in that reflection I'd sometimes mumble out loud, "I was almost killed." I often have flashbacks of the many times on the job I believe I was close to death. Fortunately, I'm still here, but there have been many others who weren't so lucky.

When you take into account the tremendous responsibility your law enforcement officers undertake every day, the training they receive, the atrocities they must bear witness to, and the tremendous job they do, it's impossible not to be grateful to the men and women who are keeping us all safe.

Even more terrifying is the many officers who are now being targeted and killed for no other reason than they are police officers. These cowardly murderers are ambushing officers oftentimes who aren't even on a call. No matter what the case, any officer who dies in the line of duty should be considered among the highest of tragedies and a threat to America's very way of life. It is the men and women in blue who prevent anarchy, chaos, and violence from overwhelming our society.

Nothing is more painful for me than a cop's funeral. One of the more recent funerals I attended happened to be one of the saddest moments of my life. Two officers from my department were working in an off-duty capacity at a private party, but they were in full uniform. One of the guests was drunk, causing problems, and was asked to leave. He refused, and the officers ended up having to physically remove him.

Unbeknownst to the officers, this made him really angry—so angry that later in the night, the man returned with a gun and shot both officers from behind. They never had a chance. One of the officers was killed instantly. The other survived. At the time of this funeral, I had been on the job for several years, and I found out the more years I had on the job, the harder these funerals became.

There wasn't enough room in the church for all the people attending this service. Outside in the street there was a sea of blue uniforms, standing at attention watching the service on giant jumbotrons, similar to the screens at a professional football stadium. The street was closed, as one of the city's biggest churches couldn't come close to housing all the attendees. Inside, the church was packed and television monitors showed the faces of the grieving family. Bagpipes played before and after the service, their melodies beautiful and haunting.

The procession stretched for miles and miles, comprised of mostly police cars with their lights flashing. Police from all over the state and all over the country had sent officers to show their respect. I was driving a detective car by myself, and I saw the most amazing thing I have ever seen. All along the route to the cemetery were citizens, but they weren't flipping us off like usual. Instead, they were holding signs of support or flags and waving. For ten miles, there were people on both sides of the road. The overpasses were jammed with citizens all showing their thanks and respect. Some people had their hands over their hearts, others saluted. It was the most magnificent sight I had ever seen. People stopped what they were doing and came out to thank the fallen officer for his sacrifice.

At the cemetery, they did the twenty-one-gun-salute and released a flock of white doves at the conclusion of the service. At this point I was so emotional I wasn't sure I could stand there much longer. I could feel the souls of not just this dead officer, but of all the others who had given their lives before him. They were at peace now, but the sorrow of the moment came from the realization that the world can be an ugly, violent place.

Evil will always be at odds with good, and the police will always be there, ready to defend people when they call. It was a moment of realization that the human race will always have among it people who are willing to hurt others, but despite all the ugliness, there are still moments of complete heroism. Moments of pure courage, valor, and selflessness will overshadow the violence and make people believe in us again.

I cried a lot that day. I'm not going to lie and say that some of my tears weren't for the fact that this could one day be me. I thought of all my co-workers who have become my family, and wondered if I would be attending another service for one of them some day. Some of the tears were for all of the officers in the past who had succumbed to the same fate. Even still, a few tears were for the kids who had to deal with the loss of their daddy, for a wife who had lost her husband, and the parents who had to bury their son. I thought of the friends, co-workers, and a community who had lost one of their own.

Sometimes all of the scenarios and training a cop gets isn't enough. If you were shot from behind, there isn't a lot you can do about it. Lots of officers are killed in the line of duty. I read about them routinely. Officers make it a habit to try to learn something from the death of a fellow officer. Some of them had no chance, but others did. This is why officers train so intensely. We are not paid to die. We are not paid to get stabbed so that the guy coming at us with the knife doesn't have to be shot.

We are paid to win, and by law, we are allowed to win decisively.

Our training is meant to help us do what we have to, and minimize the probability of injury or death to ourselves and others. There is no way to ever know the exact number of situations that were resolved safely because of training. However, it is an absolute truth that training is responsible for a great majority of peacefully resolved situations.

Inherent in the training is an assumption that almost every person has the will and intent to harm the police. That's an assumption that is critical to our survival. And, you can't run around thinking everyone is out to kill you without it changing who you are as a person.

After you've been a cop for a while and a few people have proved the assumption necessary, your outlook begins to change. Add to this—all of the violence, evil, and hatred we witness on a daily basis—and it's a whole new frame of mind. Our only goal is to go home to see our families. We want to live to fight for you another day. The goal of each day is survival, all the while knowing that today might be the day I have to make the ultimate sacrifice for a stranger.

I talk about ways I don't want to die. Plane crashes, drowning, burning, heart attacks, etc. Now that I think about it, there really isn't any way I'd *like* to go. But, if I had to go now, and I could choose, I would want it to be in the line of duty. Not because I would be famous, or a hero, or because my funeral procession would be ten miles long. It's because at least for once, people like you would stop what they were doing and come say thanks.

ABOUT THE AUTHOR

This book took over ten years to complete. Between the time this book was written and published, Steve Warneke retired with honor from the Denver Police Department to pursue other dreams. While he was a police officer, Steve was also the first openly gay radio talk show host on Denver's biggest AM station.

During his time at the department, Steve won two Emmy Awards and four Edward R Murrow awards for his work with the Denver Police Department's media relations team. He was also twice awarded the department's Distinguished Service Cross and several Official Commendations.

You can find podcasts, blog articles and more from Steve at www.SteveWarneke.com.

Made in the USA
Columbia, SC
18 April 2017